DO IT YOURSELF

50 PROJECTS BY DESIGNERS AND ARTISTS

DO IT YOURSELF

50 PROJECTS BY DESIGNERS AND ARTISTS

Thomas Bärnthaler

INTRODUCTION

Designer objects that you can make yourself? Actually, that's
a contradiction in terms. After all, the designer makes a living
by designing things for clients that can be produced industrially
and then sold. Designers who give away their designs are break-
ing the commercial chain. They are cannibalizing themselves.
As a rule, designers work unseen and only make an appearance
when the design is finished – they prefer to hold their cards close
to their chests. A designer who designs something that anyone
can go on to make is rather like an artist who shows you how
his paintings can be copied. And yet, the world of design and
the world of DIY belong inseparably together. You can't think
of one without the other. The designer is a trained person who
can do something that not everyone can do – but behind the
design stands a primordial human motivation: I can do this, and
I'm going to do it now, by myself. "Do it yourself." It's a magical
moment of self-empowerment that everyone has experienced,
both the designer who has a revolutionary chair in mind and the
do-it-yourselfer starting to tackle his or her parquet floor. Perhaps
that's why so many designers were happy to allow us, as it were,
to take a look at the cards in their hand: they love the moment
of making so much that they just want to share it.

There's a feel-good factor about making things yourself. It creates
meaning. It gives you a sense of pride. For the American socio-
logist Richard Sennett, as described in his book *The Craftsman*,
this "feeling of competence" is one of the most important sources
of emotional gratification that we can experience, as it anchors
us in reality. Manual work is an opportunity for learning a skill,
and "skill is a capacity that we develop," says Sennett: it can give
fulfillment both to the violin maker and to the software develop-
er. He believes we should view ourselves as examples of *Homo*

faber – Creative Man – and thus as happy human beings. In these times of globalization and unfettered economic growth, truly creative people are rebels.

Consumer society is full of restless stirrings. This has something to do with the yearning for individuality and authentic values in a globally standardized and homogenized world. The boom in hardware stores and the rise of DIY enthusiasts over the last few years are a clear indication of this. And the new pleasure that people are taking in making things themselves is more than a romantic taste for "retro" activities. It's a step out of immaturity. Why should I buy something when I can make a better one myself? Why shouldn't I make things, rather than buying things that other people somewhere else in the world have to produce for far too little pay? Sustainability is a question of perspective, too.

The idea of DIY was born in the last century, as an escape for those with a hankering for manual work, and a hobby for amateurs and tinkerers that sometimes raised a smile among observers. But among designers, DIY found supporters: As early as the 1930s, Gerrit Rietveld, a carpenter by trade, tried to sell wooden furniture in prefabricated pieces. Forty years on, Enzo Mari released his book *Autoprogettazione* which contained dozens of blueprints for wooden furniture of all kinds. Mari associated it with a philosophical hope in the same way as Sennett: "People encouraged to build a table with their own hands will be able to understand the thinking behind it."

Then the Internet came along and changed everything, including hobbies. Today, DIY is a broad movement that, starting in the USA, England, and Japan, continues to expand. Today's DIY enthusiasts meet on portals online where they swap instructions, they independently sell products on e-commerce sites such as

Etsy, and DIY fairs draw thousands of visitors. If you can't find any of the materials listed in this book at your local hardware store, go online to find them. There are DIY magazines, myriad Facebook groups and blogs, and various subcultures such as the technophile "Maker Movement" and the feminist-inspired "Craftivism." They are united by their openness, their desire to exchange things and ideas, and trust in the wisdom of crowds. Confining knowledge to specialists is so last century.

The journalist Chris Anderson believes he can already see a new Industrial Revolution dawning. He was editor in chief of the magazine *Wired* for several years before writing two best-sellers on new Internet business models and founding a start-up company that manufactures drones. For him, the Maker, armed with a 3-D printer, computer, and entrepreneurial ambitions, is going to be the dominant economic figure of the future. Anderson's creed runs: "We are all designers now." There may be a lot of American enthusiasm in this claim, but there's no denying the facts: even the way designers view themselves has been affected by the Internet revolution and the new production technologies.

Things are on the move: designers have long since taken the signs of the times to heart and realized that social change is an opportunity. Some designers hail the 3-D printer as emancipating. Others rave about the possibilities of open design, where cooperation counts for more than competition. It's an ethos that refuses to look down on amateurs, but instead gives them a part to play in the creative process. Design should not be a one-way street. One example of how this may turn out in actual practice can be found in the fifty do-it-yourself projects by well-known designers and artists that we have gathered together in this book.

When we initially invited designers to create something that readers could make for themselves, we embarked on an open-ended experiment. It had to be a piece of furniture, an everyday object, or something decorative. Not too difficult, and not too expensive – that was the only requirement. The response was overwhelming; with only a few exceptions, the biggest stars on the international scene didn't hesitate. These projects hark back to the origins of design, back to the workshop and the studio, where it's all about hands-on activity and improvisation. They breathe the new spirit of openness. They celebrate the simple but effective idea. Most of them can be understood as suggestions that can (and indeed should) be modified, personalized, and changed as desired. Many of these storage racks, lights, and chairs are amazingly cheap when it comes to material and production, but they are not all easy to make – unless you're prepared to get your hands dirty.

Thomas Bärnthaler
Süddeutsche Zeitung Magazin

COST
US$100/£65/€80

TABLE LAMP BY
Gesa Hansen

TIME
130 Min

PRECIOUS LIGHT

Glass cloches of the kind needed for this desk lamp can be bought on eBay or from flea markets. Gesa Hansen found hers in a Paris antique store, while the porcelain bulb fitting came from her father's toolbox. "When you make something yourself, you make this object your own, it becomes something personal. A cloche adds something special to whatever you display in it. Light looks really elegant when seen through one." Everything you need for this lamp – wire, bulb (no more than 40 watts, otherwise the heat builds up), and socket – can be found at a hardware store. You can get the wooden base assembled for you there, too.

Gesa Hansen was born in Arnsberg, Germany, and studied design at the Bauhaus University, Weimar, under Axel Kufus. After working for the celebrated architect Jean Nouvel, in 2009 she founded the furniture label The Hansen Family and, in 2011, her own design studio. She lives and works in Paris. Her award-winning wooden furniture is imbued with the clarity and sense of form native to Scandinavia (her father is the Danish designer Hans Hansen) and with a warm, functional aesthetic.

WHAT YOU NEED

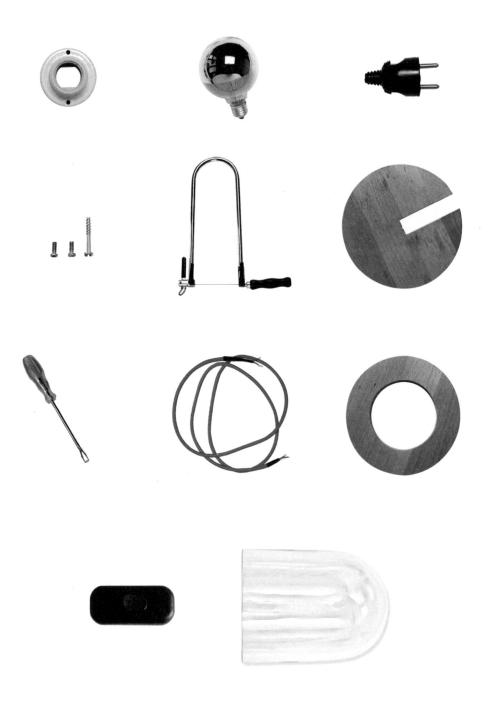

Bulb socket (with screw holes, and preferably in porcelain, as this is
more heat-resistant). Silver-coated light bulb (40 watts max).
Power plug. Screws. Fretsaw. Wooden disc (cut to shape). Screwdriver.
Cable. Wooden ring (cut to shape). Switch. Glass cloche.

INSTRUCTIONS

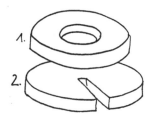

1. Measure diameters of cloche and porcelain lamp fitting.

2. Cut out two wooden discs (or someone else to do this for you). Disc 1 should be cut to the right size so the cloche will fit neatly on top; disc 2 should have a diameter approximately ¾–1 in (20–26 mm) wider and a ¾ in (20 mm) wide slit for the wire.

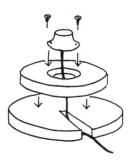

3. Connect the wire to the porcelain socket, and screw the fitting and the wooden rings together.

4. Screw in the light bulb. Connect the wire to the switch and plug.

5. Place the cloche over the assembly and plug in.

COST

US$40/£26/€35

BOOMBOX BY

Konstantin Grcic

TIME

90 Min

BOOM

There is no shortage of speakers for MP3 players and smartphones, but Konstantin Grcic has made his own particular mark in this field: "I wanted to produce something raw and cobbled together that would contrast with this polished world of gadgets." The result is a small USB box for your desk, reminiscent of an 1980s boombox and easy to set up. When you take a closer look, you'll see a face with a mouth for the center console, and the playback device like a tongue inside it. Grcic and his intern Charlotte Talbot had a whole lot of fun working on this project. "It showed us how simple things can be, even in our constrained profession."

Konstantin Grcic was born in Munich, trained as a cabinetmaker, and studied design at the Royal College of Art in London. In 1991 he set up his design studio, KGID, in Munich. His clients include firms such as Muji, Authentics, Vitra, and Magis. His Mayday lamp has been part of the Museum of Modern Art collection in New York since 2001. A 2008 poll conducted by the German *art* magazine resulted in his being named by colleagues and experts as the "greatest living designer."

WHAT YOU NEED

USB stereo speakers. Wood panels (cut to size).
Handle. Self-adhesive feet, rubber or felt. USB power adapter.
Double-sided tape (extra strength). Nails. Hammer.
Drill. Drill bits ¾, ½, and ¼ in (20, 12, and 5 mm). Pencil. Ruler.

INSTRUCTIONS

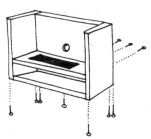

1. Measure the width and height of the two speakers together.

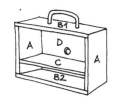

2. Cut the wooden boards to the required dimensions for your speakers.

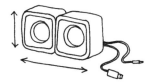
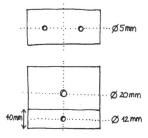

3. Bore ¼ in (5 mm) holes in the top for the handle, and ¾ in (20 mm) and ½ in (12 mm) holes in the back for the cables. Mark 1½ in (40 mm) from the bottom of the back piece to place the inside shelf.

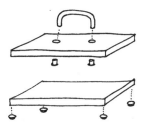

4. Mount the handle on the lid (B1) and stick the rubber or felt pads on the base (B2).

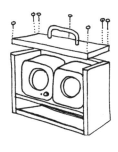

5. Nail the wooden construction together (except lid): A, B2, C, D. Attach double-sided tape to board C, pull the speaker cable through the hole, insert speakers, and fix onto the tape.

6. Nail on the lid and pull the input cable through the hole below the shelf.

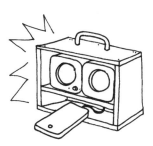

7. Attach your playback device and plug into the mains. Blast it!

EASY CHAIR 01

Easy Chair 01 is a twist on Chair 01, which Rafael Horzon designed a few years ago for his agency Redesign Deutschland. It differs in its sloped seat, which draws you into the chair. The design is captivating in its formal austerity and clarity, and consists of four equally large squares connected with screws. The boards can be cut to size in any hardware store. "The material I recommend is plywood with a top layer of birch, ½ in (12 mm) in size. This makes the chair very stable and yet amazingly light."

Rafael Horzon was born in Hamburg, and studied literature, Latin, physics, and a couple of other subjects, too, before deciding, in the mid-1990s, to "do interesting things that are different from art." He founded, for example, a scientific academy, a fashion label, and a gallery, sometimes with greater, sometimes with lesser success. His Moebel Horzon shop has become renowned beyond Berlin, as has his bookshelf Modern, which has found many customers since its release. In 2010, his autobiographical narrative *The White Book* came out.

WHAT YOU NEED

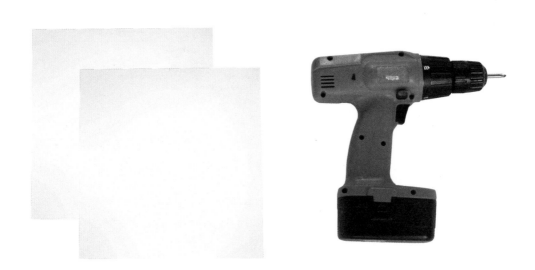

Pencil. 4 wood panels: 24 × 24 × ½ in (62 × 62 × 1.2 cm).
Cordless screwdriver. 20 wood screws.

INSTRUCTIONS

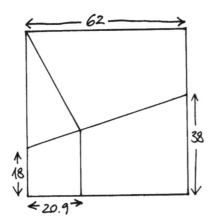

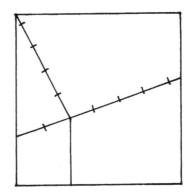

1. Draw lines on two of the four wooden boards. Mark 7 in (18 cm) from the bottom on the left, 15 in (38 cm) from the bottom on the right, and 8 in (20.9 cm) from the left on the bottom. Connect the dots!

2. Mark points spaced evenly along the lines, roughly 4 in (10 cm) apart, to position the screws.

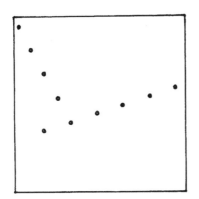

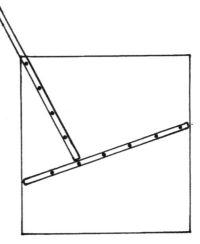

3. Bore holes.

4. Fasten the seat and back of the chair with screws.

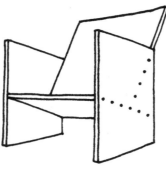

5. Relax.

COST
US$1/£1/€1

SCULPTURE BY
Sarah Sze

TIME
10 Min

PAPER ROCK

What is authentic, and what is artificial? How much can you trust your perceptions? Why do we manufacture things at all? Questions such as these go through your mind when you look at Sarah Sze's Paper Rock, a stone lump made out of crumpled paper that defies any purpose. It is very simple to make and looks deceptively real, but is neither hard, nor heavy, nor stable. It is neither a paperweight nor a door stop, though it could be – if you put a rock inside. Sze's Paper Rock is a tribute to the perfection of nature. Modern technology can simulate it, but cannot attain it.

Sarah Sze is a contemporary artist, born in Boston. Sze's work attempts to navigate and model the ceaseless proliferation of information and objects in contemporary life. Incorporating elements of painting, architecture, and installation within her sculpture, Sze investigates the value we place on objects and explores how objects ascribe meaning to the places and times we inhabit. In 2013, she represented the United States at the Fifty-fifth Venice Biennale. She lives and works in New York City.

WHAT YOU NEED

Paper. Digital camera. Rock. Printer.

INSTRUCTIONS

1. Take a close-up photograph of a rock in which the rock fills the entire frame of the photograph, or look online to find your ideal rock texture from anywhere in the world.

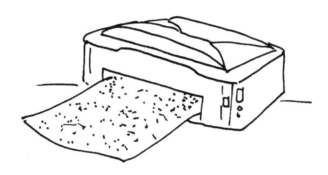

2. Print the photograph on both sides of a sheet of paper of any size.

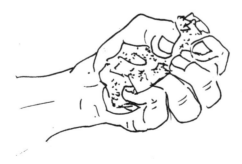

3. Crumple the piece of paper into a tight ball, keeping the top as smooth as possible.

TAPESTRY

The idea of decorating walls with carpets or other woven goods does not seem to suit our time. Minimalism reigns: bare walls, raw plaster, and cool severity instead of warmth and decoration. That these are not mutually exclusive is proven by this knotted wall decoration by the British designer Faye Toogood. It is a variation on a tapestry from her current furniture collection Assemblage 4. Out of twenty-two lengths of white rope and a lot of (uncomplicated) knotting, she has created an elegant ornament that immediately attracts attention. "This macramé knotting technique is a tradition from fisheries. Fishermen have always knotted nets like this, and created ornaments with which they decorated their ships."

Faye Toogood was born in Rutland, England. She has made a name for herself in recent years, especially with her chairs, stools, and tables, all of which look more like sculptures than pieces of furniture. After art studies, Toogood worked as a stylist, and in 2008 she founded her own interdisciplinary studio. Four years later, she received the Wallpaper Design Award. She designs products, interiors, and installations for clients such as Hermès, Montblanc, and Swarovski.

WHAT YOU NEED

Rope, 22 pieces, each 13 ft (4 m) long. Scissors.
Black electrical tape. Wooden dowel, 36 in (90 cm).
2 coathooks. Ruler or tape measure.

INSTRUCTIONS

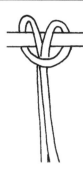

1. Cut 22 lengths of rope, each 13 ft (4 m) long, and loop them around the dowel, with the ends aligning. Space out evenly. Tie all 22 pieces of rope onto the wooden dowel with a slipknot, making sure all the ends align.

2. Attach 2 coathooks to the wall, about 28 in (70 cm) apart, then hang the dowel from the hooks.

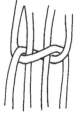 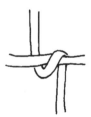 

Knot 1   Knot 2   Taping

3. Now you can follow the macramé pattern on page 212 using just the two macramé knots above, and taping as shown.

COST
US$30/£19/€26

TABLE LAMP BY
Elia Mangia

TIME
45 Min

SQUARE

This minimalist table lamp proves that it is often simple shapes, in this case a simple tool from the hardware store, that provide the starting point for impressive designs. "I found the inspiration for this lamp in the main component of the lamp itself: the steel angle. As I was walking around in a big DIY store, this red metal square, used to verify the perpendicularity between surfaces, drew my attention. It was a very simple, rigorous, and strong object, yet colorful, cheerful, and very cheap! A beautiful object I would have liked to keep on my desk. I just had to find a new function for it! The transition was immediate."

Elia Mangia was born in Milan. He studied industrial design at St. Martin's College in London and at the Istituto Europeo di Design in Milan. In 2007, he founded his own design studio in Milan, which counts firms such as Ligne Roset, Nespresso, Saeco, and Bosa among its customers. He became famous with Critter, a mobile, free-standing kitchen for the Skitsch company. Since 2008 he has also taught industrial design in Milan.

WHAT YOU NEED

Metal square. Wooden block, 19½ in (49.5 cm) long. Bolt and wing nut.
Magnets, ⅜ and ½ in (10 and 12 mm) diameter. Plug and switch.
20 watt bi-pin halogen bulb with G8 base. G8 bulb socket. Electric cable.
Superglue. Saw. Drill. Drill bit, ¼ in (6 mm).

Spade bits, ⅜ and ½ in (10 and 12 mm), plus one the width of the socket.

INSTRUCTIONS

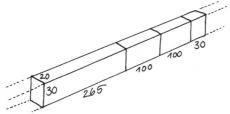

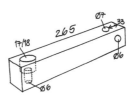

1. Cut the wooden baton into four parts. One 10½ in (265 mm), two 4 in (100 mm), and one 1 in (30 mm) long.

2. Drill holes for the G8 socket and cable, about ¾ in and ¼ in (18 mm and 6 mm) in this case, according to the diagram.

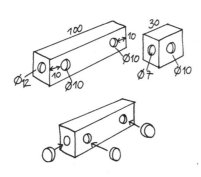

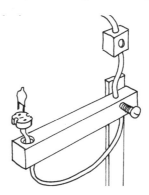

3. Use the spade bits to make holes for the magnets, and glue the magnets in.

4. Fix the cable to the bulb socket and run through the holes in the arm and the smallest wooden block. Screw on the arm of the lamp with the bolt and wing nut.

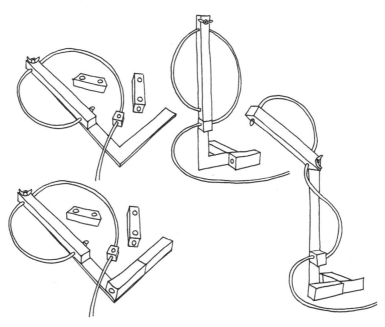

5. Use the two remaining magnetic blocks to set up the lamp so that it does not tip over.

COST
US$120/£70/€90

SHELVES BY
Sebastian Herkner

TIME
360 Min

TRANSIT

Sebastian Herkner's shelves will go in a living room or a kitchen, but also in a studio or workshop. They're plain, but they can be easily modified: "My intention was to design a set of shelves using clamps so that they wouldn't seem static and pre-programmed, but would suit the changing needs of the user. Shelves have to do more than provide space for books or tools: they're a place where you can exhibit memories and things of personal value." The individual shelves can be moved or mounted upside down. The clamps make a flexible construction possible, with many variations.

Sebastian Herkner studied product design in Offenbach am Main, Germany. There, in 2006, he founded his own design studio, and since then has been working as a designer for clients such as ClassiCon, De Vorm, Rosenthal, and Moroso; he also works as a guest lecturer. His designs have won numerous awards. In 2011, he won the German national design prize in the "new blood" category.

WHAT YOU NEED

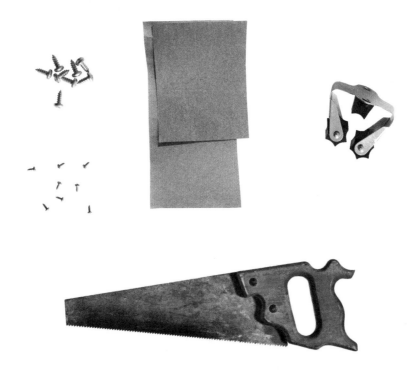

Nails. Wood screws. Sandpaper.
26 broom clamps. Saw.
6 broomsticks, 1 in (25 mm) diameter.
Birch plywood, ⅜ in (9 mm) thick.

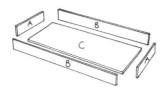

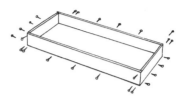

1. The following birch plywood boards are needed – Shelf 1: A: 2½ × 10 in (6.5 × 25.5 cm); B: 2½ × 24 in (6.5 × 61 cm); C: 23¼ × 10 in (59 × 25.5 cm). Shelf 2: A: 4 × 10 in (10 × 25.5 cm); B: 4 × 24 in (10 × 61 cm); C: 23¼ × 10 in (59 × 25.5 cm).

2. Make a shelf from pieces A, B, and C. First glue and then nail them together. Varnish in whatever color is desired.

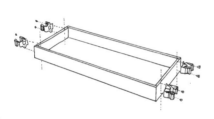

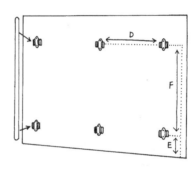

3. Attach clamps to the short sides (A) of the shelf with corresponding wooden screws. The clamps must be aligned precisely vertically. Four clamps are needed for each shelf. Clamps should lie flush with the shelf.

4. The clamps are attached to the wall as follows: D = length of shelf L + 2 in (5 cm) [here: 26 in (66 cm)], E = 8 in (20 cm), F = total height – 8 in (20 cm) [here: 39 in (99 cm)]. Finally, attach the shelf racks to the wall mounts.

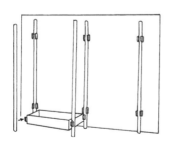

5. Now you can assemble the modules as you wish.

6. The shelves can also be turned upside down – that is, used as flat shelves or as containers.

COST
US$50/£33/€44

HOOK & LEDGE BY
Daniel Emma

TIME
120 Min

HOOK & LEDGE

Following their motto and making things that are "just nice," this Australian design couple created a ledge that is as plain as possible and yet highly remarkable. As in their prize-winning desk items, they employ exclusively geometric forms. Hook & Ledge consists of a hook module and a small ledge. "The idea was to create an object that was practical, good for everyday purposes, and useful." Keys, little flasks of perfume, photos, and other odds and ends can find a place on this rectangular ledge. The number of cylindrical hooks can be increased as desired.

Daniel To and Emma Aiston both trained as industrial designers and founded their design studio Daniel Emma in 2008 in Adelaide, Australia, after working in London for, among others, Marc Newson. Their designs are guided by simple geometrical forms and have many references to their native land. They achieved worldwide renown with "D.E.," a collection of attractive desk items. In 2010, they won the Bombay Sapphire Award, Australia's most important design prize.

WHAT YOU NEED

Metal handsaw. Block of wood 4 × 4 × 20 in (10 × 10 × 51 cm).
2 wooden poles, ¾ and 1½ in (20 and 45 mm) diameter. Wood glue.
Spray paint. 3 magnets, ⅜ in (10 mm) diameter. Drill. Forstner bit,
1½ in (45 mm). Drill bits, ⅜ and ¼ in (10 and 5 mm).
Wall screws with dowels.

INSTRUCTIONS

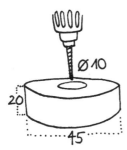

1. Take the 1½ in (45 mm) wooden pole and cut off a piece ¾ in (20 mm) long. Bore a ⅜ in (10 mm) hole into the middle.

2. Cut off another three ¼ in (5 mm) long pieces from this pole. Spray paint with desired color. These will later be used as cover plates.

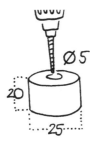

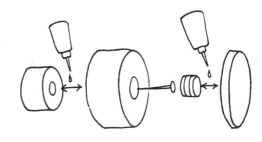

3. Take the ¾ in (20 mm) wooden pole and cut off a piece ¾ in (20 mm) long. In the middle bore a ¼ in (5 mm) hole.

4. Glue the pieces of the hook together and screw to the wall; glue the magnets to the cover plates and attach the cover plates.

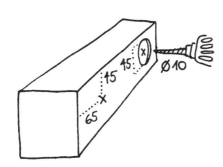

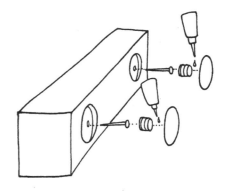

5. Draw holes for boring on the console as shown: 2½ in (65 mm) from each end. Use the ⅜ in (10 mm) bit to bore approximately 1¼ in (35 mm) deep holes, then bore through with the ¼ in (5 mm) bit. Use the forstner bit to cut two ¼ in (5 mm) deep stud holes.

6. Screw the ledge to the wall, glue the magnets to the painted cover plates, and attach the cover plates.

LIGHTNUM

Wood is the main material required for building this candle holder, which is intended to be a table decoration. "The name is derived from the Latin *lignum*, meaning wood," says Alfredo Häberli. "I wanted to design something that looks celebratory and yet practical, and is easy to use in different ways." Candles with different diameters can be mounted thanks to the strap attachments, and set up at varying heights either symmetrically or in more random groups. Please ensure you remember the cut-out label! It reads: Do not leave burning unattended!

Alfredo Häberli was born in Buenos Aires and emigrated to Switzerland in 1977. There he studied industrial design at the Höhere Schule für Gestaltung. Currently he runs a design studio in Zürich. His motto is: "Design must not be obtrusive." He designs for firms such as Moroso, Volvo, and Luceplan. His "Origo" tableware for Iittala was awarded the iF Product Design Award in 2002.

WHAT YOU NEED

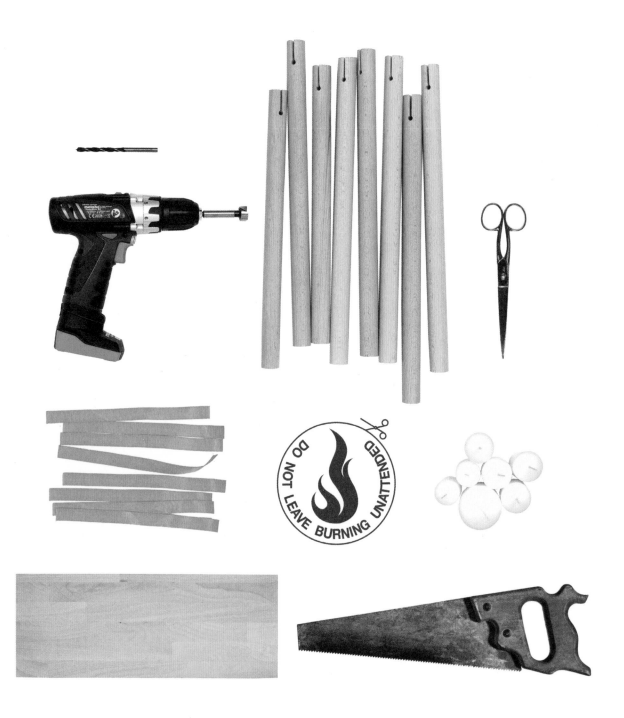

Drill bits ¼ and ¾ in (5 and 20 mm) and drill.
8 rods, ¾ in (2 cm) diameter, 12 in (320 mm) long.
Scissors. Strong nylon ribbon. Warning label.
Candles. Board 23 × 9 × ¾ in (58 × 22 × 2 cm). Saw.

INSTRUCTIONS

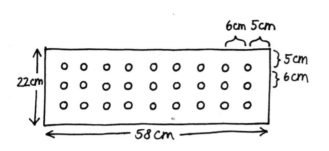

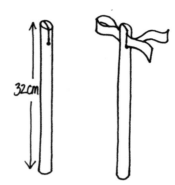

1. Bore holes for the rods in the wooden board evenly, about 2 in (6cm) apart throughout, starting 2 in (5 cm) from the edge.

2. Bore a ¼ in (5 mm) hole 1 in (25 mm) from the top of each rod; cut a slit down to the hole.

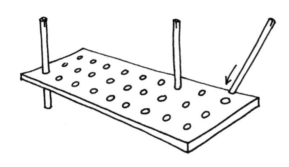

3. Insert rods in the holes as you wish, but ensure that the board is stable and level.

4. Attach candles with ribbons and pull tight.

5. Attach the warning label. Light the candles. When the candle burns down to the ribbon, change it!

COST
US$50/£33/€44

PENDANT LIGHT BY
Nils Holger Moormann

TIME
150 Min

BRANCH LAMP

Nils Holger Moormann spent a long time trying to find a lamp for his conference room, but couldn't find anything suitable. Then, one day, a storm blew a fine branch into his yard. "It suddenly all clicked! Since that time, a lot of visitors have asked me how they can make their own branch lamps. The essential thing you need is a fine branch, the kind you're most likely to find on a long hike through the woods. And please – use nice, dimmable lighting, none of those off-the-rack energy-efficient bulbs." Moormann also recommends that you look for nice cords that suit the material or have a pattern. "That means you'll have a shining example of the way technology and nature can come together."

Nils Holger Moormann interrupted his law studies in 1982 and, teaching himself the process, began to produce furniture for young designers. Now fifty-nine years old, and having won several awards, his breakthrough came with the Taut Shelving designed for Wolfgang Laubersheimer. Since 1992, his design studio in Aschau im Chiemgau, Germany, has followed the motto "Simplicity, intelligence, and innovation."

WHAT YOU NEED

Beautiful branch. Power cords (length depending on ceiling height and number
of desired bulbs). Bulbs. Bulb sockets. Wall anchors. Screw hooks.
Screw terminals (also depending on number of bulbs).

INSTRUCTIONS

1. Determine how many light sources and lengths of cord you want. Attach the cables to the bulb sockets.

2. Attach anchors and screw hooks to the ceiling in the desired places to hang the lights.

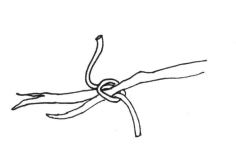

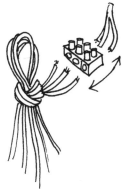

3. Knot the electric cords around the branches.

4. Gather the ends leading to the ceiling and knot them in a loop. Attach the cords to the electrical power supply with the screw terminals.

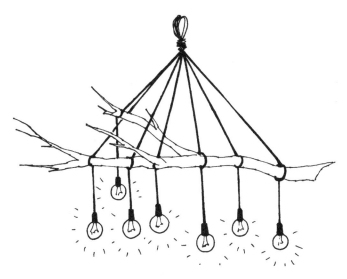

5. Hang the knotted cords from the hooks. Screw in the light bulbs.

COST
US$30/£19/€26

SHIRT RACK BY
Antenna Design

TIME
90 Min

HANGOUT

Designers are all about developing solutions to problems. For their DIY project, Masamichi Udagawa and Sigi Moeslinger of Antenna Design took the opposite route: "We went to a hardware store and were inspired by what was on offer." They bought a broomstick and a colorful rope and let their assistants Isaac Chen and Binsei Numao experiment. The result is a valet stand of remarkable simplicity. The rope is passed through drill holes in the stem and then laterally anchored in the wall so that the construction casually hangs into the room. Perfect for bedrooms or unused corners in shared apartments.

Masamichi Udagawa from Tokyo and Sigi Moeslinger from Vienna founded Antenna Design in New York in 1997. Their mission: to make everyday objects more beautiful. Their portfolio ranges from metro trains and ticket machines to furniture and flat screens. Udagawa publishes in international design magazines. He and Moeslinger have won several awards and share their experience with their students at Yale University.

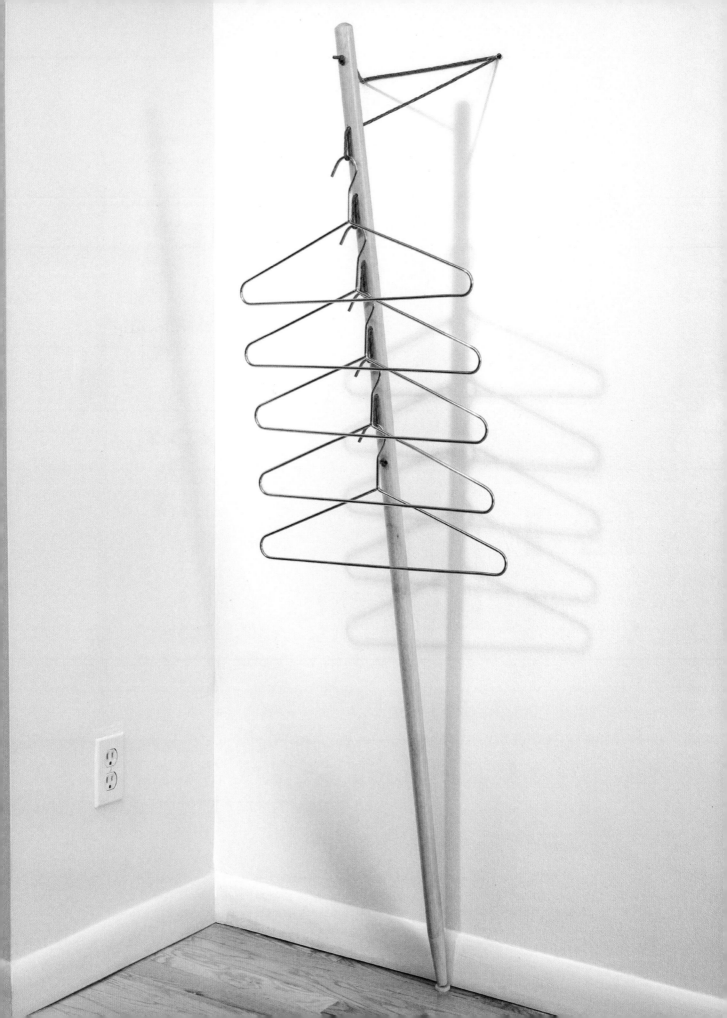

WHAT YOU NEED

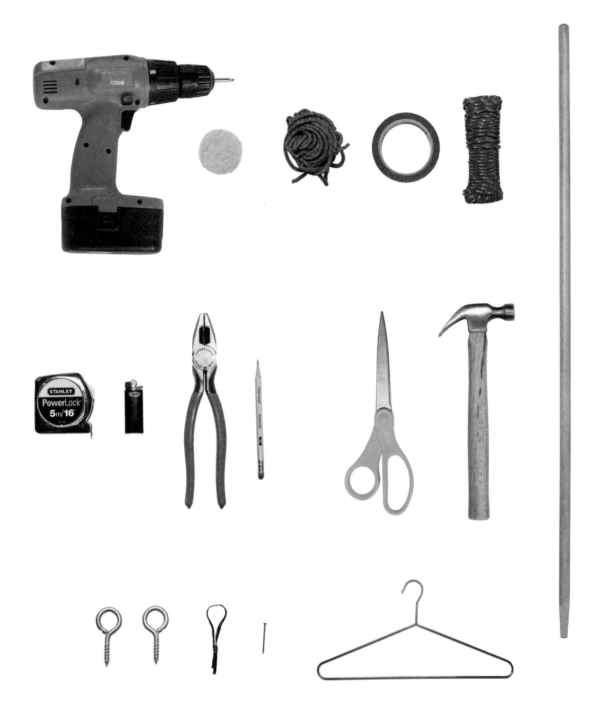

Drill. Drill bits ⅛ and ¼ in (3 and 6 mm). Round felt pad, 45 mm.
Colored rope, 96½ in (245 cm) long and ¼ in (7 mm) thick. Tape.
Tape measure. Lighter. Pliers. Pencil. Scissors. Hammer. Broomstick.
2 eye screws, big enough for the rope. Twist tie. Nail, 1 in (25 mm).
5 wire hangers.

INSTRUCTIONS

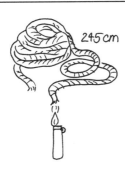

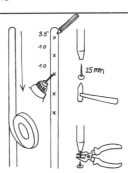

1. Cut 96½ in (245 cm) of rope. Use the lighter to harden the ends of the rope.

2. Mark seven holes, 4 in (10 cm) apart, starting the first hole 1½ in (3.5 cm) from the top of the broomstick. Use tape to cover and mark locations before drilling, for clean holes. Use ⅛ in (3 mm) drill bit for pilot holes, ¼ in (6 mm) for actual holes.

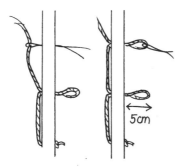

3. Knot one end of the rope and feed it through the lowest hole. Using a twist tie, pull the rope through each hole to form loops. Keep the rope taut. The length of each loop should be about 2 in (5 cm). Make five loops. Pull the remaining rope through two eye screws.

4. Pull the rope through the final top hole and knot the end. Hammer the nail into the bottom of the broomstick, leaving about ½ in (10 mm) exposed.

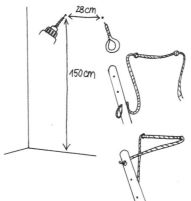

5. Drill two holes 11 in (28 cm) apart and 59 in (150 cm) from the floor (depending on the length of the broomstick). Place the felt pad on the floor, centered between the holes. Fix the eye screws and the broomstick onto the wall, placing the nail on the felt pad. Center the broomstick between the eye screws.

53

COST
US$35/£22/€30

TABLEWARE BY
Stephen Burks

TIME
180 Min

PAILLETTES

This object has two faces: Depending on the way you present it, it can be either a bowl or a vase. There's nothing so surprising in this, as both of the two most important elements in it are a glass vase and a glass bowl, of the kind you can find in any kitchen cupboard, at a flea market, or at IKEA. The trick lies in combining them. To produce a patchwork pattern like the one in the picture, you need a piece of attractive oilcloth, a pair of scissors to cut out the *paillettes,* or "sequins", and a supply of epoxy or decoupage medium. An original, spontaneous work of art will emerge – a "readymade," as designer Stephen Burks would say.

Stephen Burks initially studied architecture in Chicago and New York, but then became an industrial designer and, in 1997, set up his own studio, Stephen Burks Man Made. Burks's products grapple with themes such as sustainability, globalization, and craft. His work for Cappellini, Moroso, and Audi has won several awards. He lives and works in New York.

WHAT YOU NEED

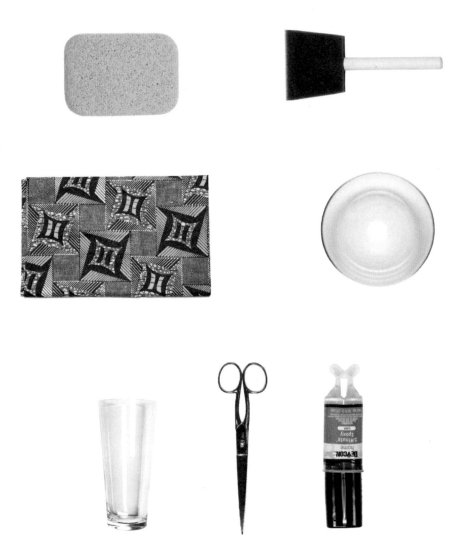

Sponge. Foam brush.
Oilcloth. Glass bowl.
Tall glass vase. Scissors. Water-soluble epoxy.

INSTRUCTIONS

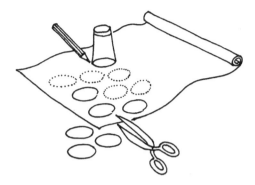

1. Using the bottom of the vase, draw circular "sequins" on the oilcloth, and cut them out.

2. Glue the sequins in an overlapping pattern onto the vase and glass. Use water-soluble glue or decoupage medium.

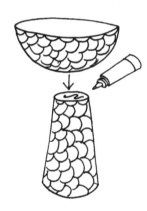

3. Smooth down the surfaces with a damp sponge.

4. Glue the bowl and vase together.

5. Fill with whatever you desire. The object can be used as a bowl or a vase.

COST
US$7/£5/€6

CHAIR BY
Martino Gamper

TIME
120 Min

PALETTE

When we asked Martino Gamper for a DIY design, he was traveling in New Zealand. But that didn't stop him from creating one of the DIY chairs that he is famous for being able to put together out of bits and pieces he comes across — and he did so in just a few hours. His basic material was a European pallet, the kind you can run up just about anywhere — even on the other side of the world! (The "European" pallet is defined as a wooden pallet with five long slats across the top.) "You can get standard pallets at almost any discount store, in markets, or in warehouses. You can often pick them up for free. Putting this chair together was a nice bit of practice for me; I did it in my in-laws' garden."

Martino Gamper straddles the divide between art and design, and is seen as an individualist who suspects that humor is more important than the dogma of functionality. Even when he was still studying with Ron Arad at the Royal College of Art, his work was interdisciplinary in nature. Now he designs exhibitions and art installations, teaches, and works for companies such as Magis and Moroso. Born in Italy, he lives and works in London.

Wooden European pallet. Nails.
Saw. Hammer.
Tape measure. Sandpaper.

INSTRUCTIONS

1. Remove the two outer slats of the pallet.

2. Saw up the pallet as shown.

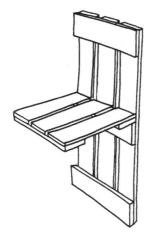

3. The seat is placed against the middle brace and nailed into it from behind.

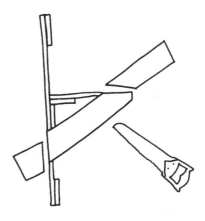

4. Use the remaining slats to saw up struts for the seat, and nail or screw them together.

5. Sand down the rough edges.

FLOATING FOREST

The idea for these three glass germinators came to Michael Anastassiades when he saw a vase by the Swedish designer Estrid Ericson, in which you could leave acorns to germinate over the winter: "I loved the simple poetry of this object. It embodied the hope for early spring, especially coming from a country with such heavy and dark winters." Anastassiades's three variations on the design fix an acorn or avocado pit in a glass vase in such a way that the pit floats as upright as possible on the water, so you can watch it for weeks on end, budding and growing, until it is finally strong enough to plant.

Michael Anastassiades, born in Cyprus in 1967, is best known for his lighting and furnishings that adorn hotels, restaurants, shops, and homes all around the world. His designs for clients such as FLOS, Swarovski, and the V&A Museum in London always spill over the boundaries between industrial design, sculpture, and the decorative arts. Anastassiades lives in London, where he has run his own design studio since 1994.

WHAT YOU NEED

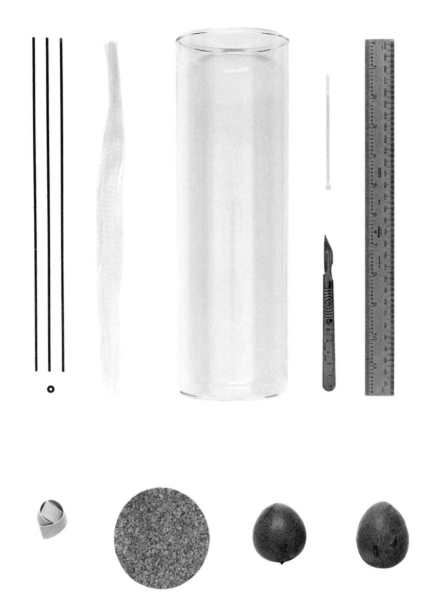

Metal rods. Rubber ring. Garlic net. Glass vase. Small zip tie. Cutter. Ruler.
Rubber band. Cork pad. Acorn. Avocado pit.

INSTRUCTIONS

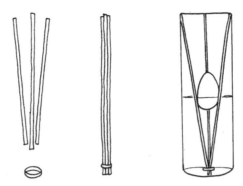

Version 1: Fix three metal rods with a rubber ring and place centrally in the vase so that they spread apart into a pyramid. Place the avocado pit and fill the vase with water so that the pit is half covered.

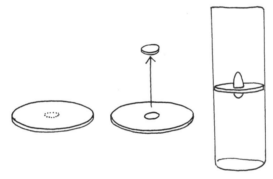

Version 2: Cut the cork pad so that it fits into the vase and floats on the water. In the middle, cut a hole for the acorn. Insert the acorn and fill the vase with water.

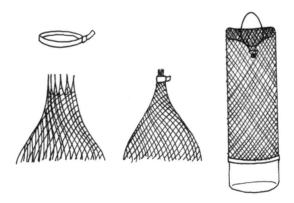

Version 3: Put the garlic net over the vase. Bind the net on top with a zip tie. Put the net over the vase so that the avocado pit sits in it. Fill up to the pit with water.

COST
US$50/£33/€44

WALL LIGHT BY
Team Ingo Maurer

TIME
60 Min

YOURSELF

This lamp will go well on a table, next to the bed, or behind a wingback chair. It can be placed above, to one side, or standing away from the wall. The main element is a neoprene squeegee, fixed onto a broomstick. "The idea of designing a simple product that could be put together at home but didn't look like a DIY piece appealed to us. The beauty of supposedly ordinary everyday objects often doesn't reveal itself until you take them out of their usual context and discover new functions in them." That's true of this lamp, too: If the bathtub happens to overflow, you can also use it to mop the floor.

Team Ingo Maurer is Ingo Maurer's "working family": fourteen designers, architects, artists, and autodidacts who produce and develop ideas and designs for Ingo Maurer. Ingo Maurer is one of the most influential lighting designers of the present day. His Bulb light was made part of the permanent collection of the Museum of Modern Art in New York in 1969. In 2010, the Federal Republic of Germany awarded him its design prize for his life's work.

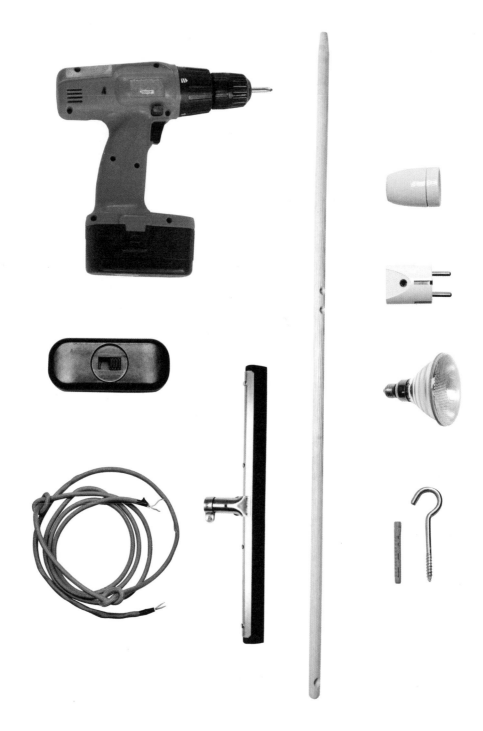

Drill. Broomstick. Socket. Power plug. Switch.
Cable. Neoprene squeegee. PAR38 bulb. Wall anchors. Screw hooks.

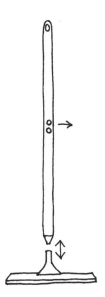

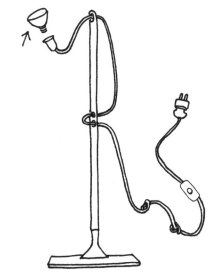

1. Bore two holes of the same diameter as the electric cable into the middle of the broomstick.

2. Pull a cable approximately 12 ft (4 m) long through both holes. Knot the cable twice, about 24 in (60 cm) from the broomstick. Attach socket, switch, and plug.

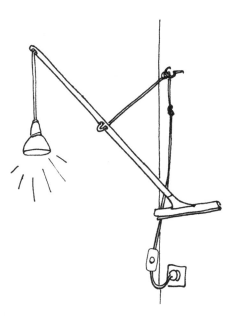

3. Screw a hook into the wall, hang up the lamp as shown, screw in the bulb, and turn on.

COST
US$5/£3/€4

SOAP BY
John Baldessari

TIME
5 Min

A LARGE PIECE OF SOAP BECOMES A SMALL PIECE OF SOAP EVENTUALLY

Humor is a powerful force in the arts. Marcel Duchamp had it, Martin Kippenberger had it, and of course John Baldessari – the great Californian conceptual artist and creator of this piece – has it. They all care little for genre boundaries and laugh at art that takes itself too seriously. Baldessari created this project in collaboration with fellow artist Molly Berman. Carving a hole in a bar of soap so that it escapes the fate of becoming leftover soap that you throw away could be a quip about our rampant consumer culture. But it also shows that the design of bars of soap suffers from an inherent defect.

 John Baldessari was born in National City, California. He attended San Diego State University and did postgraduate work at Otis College of Art and Design. Baldessari's artwork, which spans painting, photography, printmaking, film, installation, and sculpture, has been featured in more than two hundred solo exhibitions in the United States and Europe. In 2009, he was awarded the Golden Lion at the Venice Biennale, the art world's highest honor. He lives and works in California.

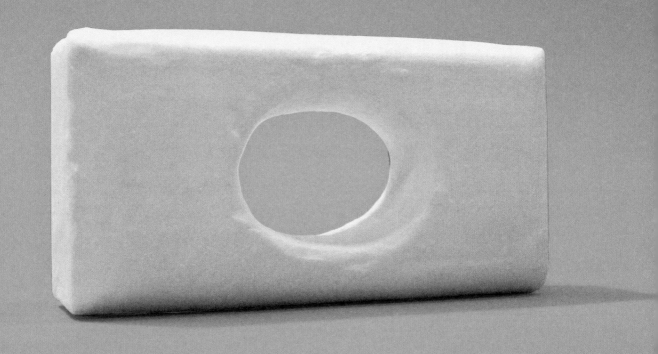

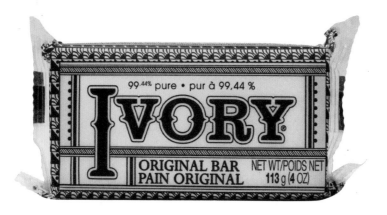

Soap. Knife.

INSTRUCTIONS

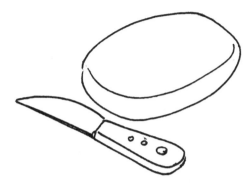

1. Pick up the knife. Pick up the soap.

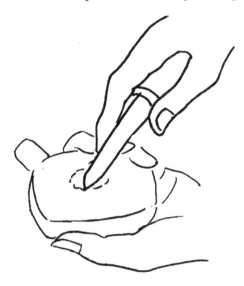

2. Cut a hole in the soap.

3. Smile.

COST
US$40/£26/€35

TABLE LAMP BY
Jean-Marie Massaud

TIME
20 Min

MAGNETO

A small shovel usually doesn't get to see much light. Its world is the dark coal cellar, amid the soot and dust. But certainties such as these have never deterred the French designer and architect Jean-Marie Massaud from questioning them. He found all the parts for this lamp in the household appliances section of the Paris department store BHV. In his design, thanks to two magnets connected by a hinge, the shovel is turned into a lampshade and thus, contrary to its nature, becomes a giver of light. It's as if its special shape were tailor-made for the purpose. Of course, you can also use any other type of metal dustpan for this table lamp.

Jean-Marie Massaud was born in Toulouse, France. Since the beginning of his career in 1990, he has worked on an extensive range of projects, stretching from stadiums to furniture, from one-off projects to serial ones, from macro-environments to micro-contexts. Major brands such as Axor, Cassina, Poliform, and Toyota have called on his ability to mix comfort and elegance, zeitgeist and heritage, generosity and distinction. He lives and works in Paris.

GYS double articulated magnetic positioner.
LED plate and transformer. Plug. Iron coal shovel.
Metal plate, 4 × 4 × ¼ in (100 × 100 × 6 mm). Cable.
Superglue. Screwdriver. Cutter. Drill. Drill bit for iron, ¼ in (6 mm).

INSTRUCTIONS

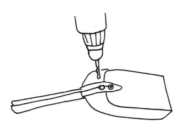

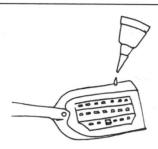

1. Drill a hole in the shovel that is big enough to pass the wire through.

2. Glue the LEDs to the inside of the shovel.

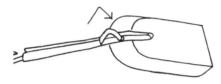

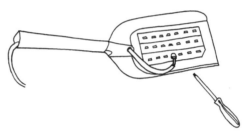

3. Pass the power cable through the opening of the handle and through the hole drilled before.

4. Connect the power cable with the LEDs.

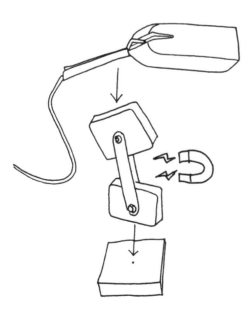

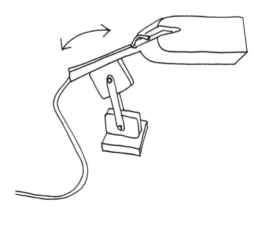

5. Join the shovel to the magnets and place both on the metal sheet.

6. The lamp is ready to use and easy to adjust in height and position.

COST
US$60/£40/€53

DESK ORGANIZER BY
Ladies & Gentlemen

TIME
90 Min

PLAYSCAPE

Playscape represents a core part of L&G's design process: Many of their products are conceived serendipitously by arranging blocks of material samples in ways that create unexpected harmonies. Playscape is one such experiment. All the materials can be found at hardware and craft stores. The abstract and austere forms work together to create a surprisingly warm functional object, while still celebrating elemental materials and geometries. The combination creates a flexible platform to store and display common objects on a tabletop, vanity, or desktop. DIYers are invited to consider their own composition by changing the arrangement, sizing, or materials to suit their whims and needs.

Ladies & Gentlemen is a Seattle-based design studio creating small objects, home goods, jewelry, furniture, lighting, and more. Founded by Dylan Davis and Jean Lee in 2010, the studio's explorations in materiality blend their curiosity with the desire to find unexpected pairings of material and function. Their multidisciplinary approach to design yields an ever-evolving set of ideas and experiments collected from their everyday discoveries and surroundings.

WHAT YOU NEED

Marble tile, 12 × 12 in (30.5 × 30.5 cm). Wooden sphere, 2½ in (6.5 cm) diameter.
Wooden disc, ¾ in (2 cm) high × 2⅜ in (6 cm) diameter.
Copper or brass tubing, 4 in (10 cm) long × 2½ in (6.5 cm) diameter.
Brass keystock, 5 × ⅜ × ⅜ in (127 × 9 × 9 mm). Fine steel wool.
Wooden cone, 3 in (7.5 cm) high, 2 in (5 cm) diameter.
150 grit wet/dry sandpaper. Button head wood screws with small washers,
1 in (2 cm) long. 3 wood screws, ¾ in (2 cm) long.
Rag. Small rubber feet. Epoxy. Tray wide enough to fit tile.
Hacksaw. Pencil. Screwdriver. Drill. Masonry bit, ⅜ in (9 mm).

INSTRUCTIONS

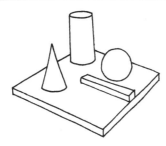

1. Use a hacksaw and cut the metal tubing, square brass keystock, and wooden dowel to the specified lengths – or have the hardware store do it for you.

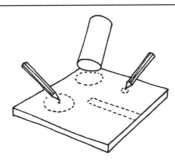

2. Sand the cut edges of the metal until smooth, and sand the bottom of the wooden sphere so that it has at least a ¾ in (2 cm) diameter flat area that can sit on the tile. If necessary, also sand the round disc sides until the disc fits snugly inside the metal tubing. Polish the metal surfaces with fine steel wool.

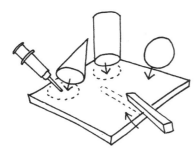

3. Arrange the pieces on the tile to create your own ideal composition – though the wooden sphere should stay 1 in (2.5 cm) to either side of the brass keystock. Outline the shapes with a pencil on the tile. Then mark the centers for the cone, sphere, and disc on the tile.

4. Submerge the tile in water in the tray, and use the masonry bit to drill the marked holes. Drill slowly from the glossy side of the marble down, stopping occasionally to make sure the bit stays wet and doesn't overheat. Then wet sand the edges to remove small chips and saw marks. Clean and dry the tile surfaces.

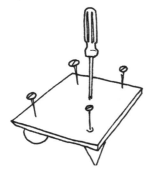

5. From the bottom of the marble tile, screw the shapes in place. Take the metal tubing and put it over the wooden disc.

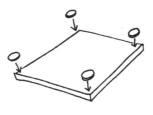

6. Epoxy the keystock in the outline marked previously. Epoxy the copper tube to the disc if desired. Place the rubber bumper feet on the underside of the tile.

COST

US$20/£13/€17

WALL CLOCK BY
Nitzan Cohen

TIME

60 Min

IT'S ABOUT TIME

Clocks run our lives, and force them into a global mold. They tick the same everywhere: on our wrists, on the bedside table, in the railway station. As a rebellion against this standardization, Nitzan Cohen has designed a minimalistic clock that is meant to spur us on to find our own individual rhythms. "Our time is never universal but always personal, so you can shape this clock in accordance with your own needs," says Cohen. It consists of just two elements, a simple clockwork mechanism and an hour hand designed by Cohen. People can then design their own clock faces. So there shouldn't be any questions about assembling it, except one: What makes you tick?

Nitzan Cohen was born in the Hazorea kibbutz in Israel, studied design in Tel Aviv and Eindhoven, and worked as a project leader in Konstantin Grcic's studio. In 2007, he set up the Nitzan Cohen studio in Munich, in pursuit of a multidisciplinary and anticonsumerist approach. Among his clients are manufacturers such as Authentics, the BMW Group, Diesel, Konica Minolta, and Thomas/Rosenthal. He teaches industrial design at the Saar College of Fine Arts in Saarbrücken.

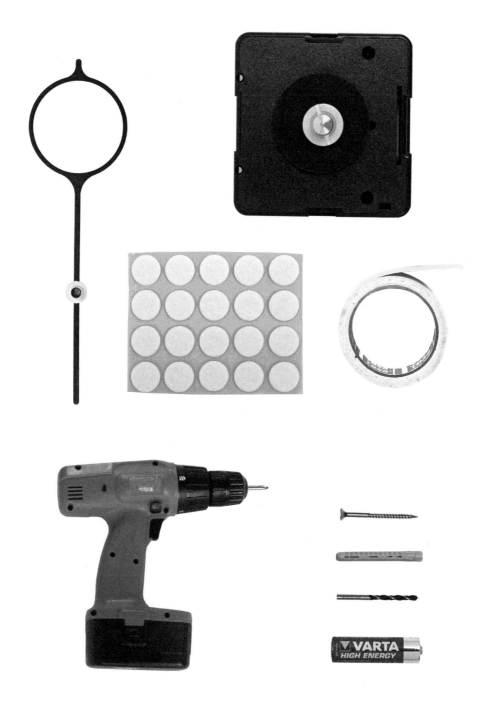

Clock finger (from shapeways.com, search term: Nitzan Cohen).
Clockwork. Felt pads. Double-sided adhesive tape. Drill.
Screw. Anchor. AA battery.

INSTRUCTIONS

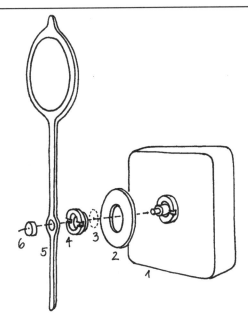

Make the clock base:

1. Clockwork
2. Washer
3. Clock face (your own design)
4. Screw
5. Hour hand
6. Cap, replaceable by second hand

1. Bore a hole in the place where you want to hang the clock.

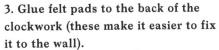

2. Mount the anchor and screw into the wall; screw head should be ¼ in (5 mm) from wall.

3. Glue felt pads to the back of the clockwork (these make it easier to fix it to the wall).

4. Alternatively, a flexible hanging is possible: You just cut a piece of double-sided adhesive and position it on the back of the clockwork.

5. Make your own clock face/background; you can find help for positioning and marking the clock at nitzan-cohen.com. Mount the clock face.

FATTO DI GIORNO

This floor lamp is Ross Lovegrove's homage to the Italian designer Ettore Sottsass, cofounder of the Memphis movement. It consists of six plastic buckets, which are connected via cable ties and a neon tube. The greenish yellow light is refreshingly cool, and the bold form is a tribute to the playful use of styles and shapes of the Memphis Group. *Fatto di giorno* means "made in a day." Lovegrove says, "This is what I do when I can just create reflexively, just go out, see, and do completely independently. It's the readymade culture that I believe all designers should take to heart right through their creative lives because it liberates the mind from calculation and is more akin to art in its spontaneity and singular voice."

Ross Lovegrove was born in Cardiff, Wales. He received his master's in design from the Royal College of Art, London, in 1983. His works range from Walkmans for Sony and computers for Apple to furniture, cameras, cars, trains, and architecture. He has won numerous international awards, and his work has been extensively published and exhibited, including in the Museum of Modern Art and Guggenheim Museum in New York, and the Design Museum, London.

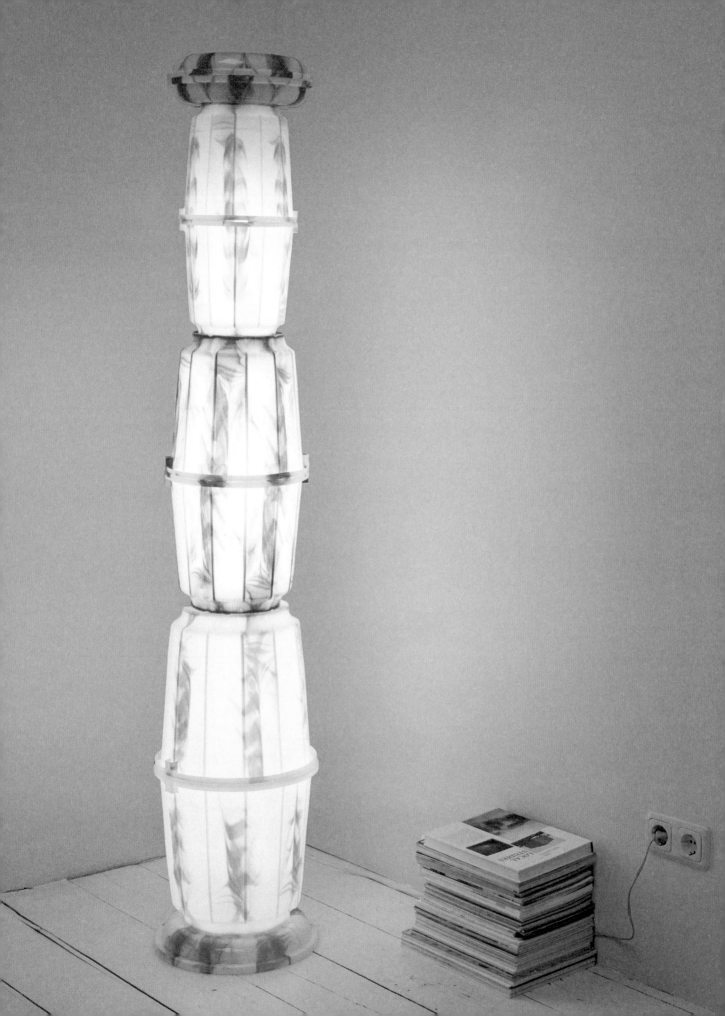

WHAT YOU NEED

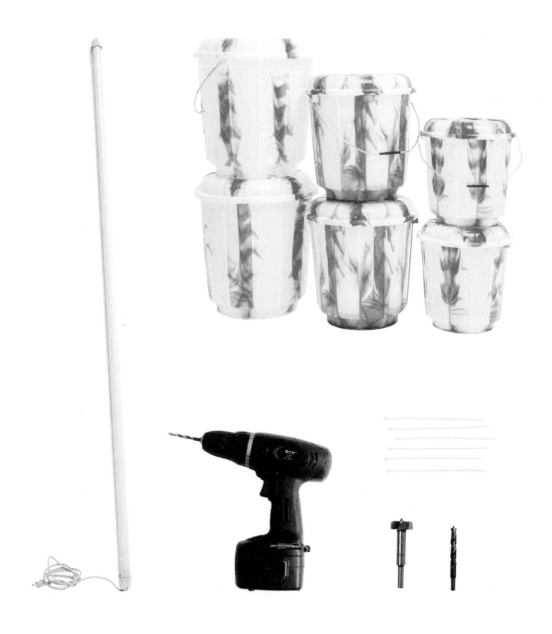

Neon tube, 67 in (170 cm). 6 multicolored plastic buckets with lids,
2 small (2 gallons or 7 liters), 2 medium (3½ gallons or 13 liters),
2 large (5½ gallons or 20 liters).
Zip ties. Drill. Forstner bit as wide as neon tube. Drill bit.

INSTRUCTIONS

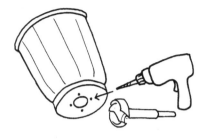

1. Remove the handles from the buckets.

2. Cut into the center of the base of the buckets holes big enough for the neon tube to be drawn through. Drill 4 holes every ¾ to 1¼ in (2 to 3 cm) around the holes in the bases for the cable ties that will hold the buckets together.

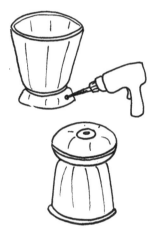

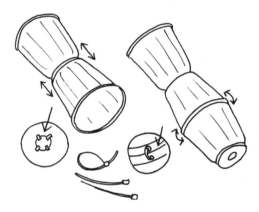

3. Drill a hole in the lid through which the power cable will be fed.

4. Put the lamp together and fix the buckets with the zip ties. Two covers act as the cap, one as a stand.

5. Feed the cable and neon rod into the lamp. Connect the rod to the mains.

COST
US$80/£50/€70

CHAIR BY
Christoph Böninger

TIME
90 Min

CART CHAIR

The idea for his chair came to Christoph Böninger from a photo of an Afghan villager sitting backward in a wheelbarrow. "I was so dazzled by the idea, and the man looked so amazingly relaxed, that I just had to try it out straightaway." The chair is made out of the tub of a wheelbarrow, screwed onto a wooden frame. You can get the wheelbarrow tub and the strips of wood from a hardware or garden store. A blanket as a backrest and a cushion to sit on will complete the chair. Excellent as a piece of garden furniture (weather-resistant!), it also works well as an eye-catching item in a living room.

Christoph Böninger studied industrial design in Munich and environmental design in Los Angeles. In 1982, he designed the first laptop in the world, now displayed in the Pinakothek der Moderne in Munich. For many years he worked for Siemens, while at the same time designing furniture, including tables for ClassiCon. He published the book *Form:Ethik*, and in 2010, together with some friends, he set up the Auerberg firm, a "product lab outside industrial norms and established fashions."

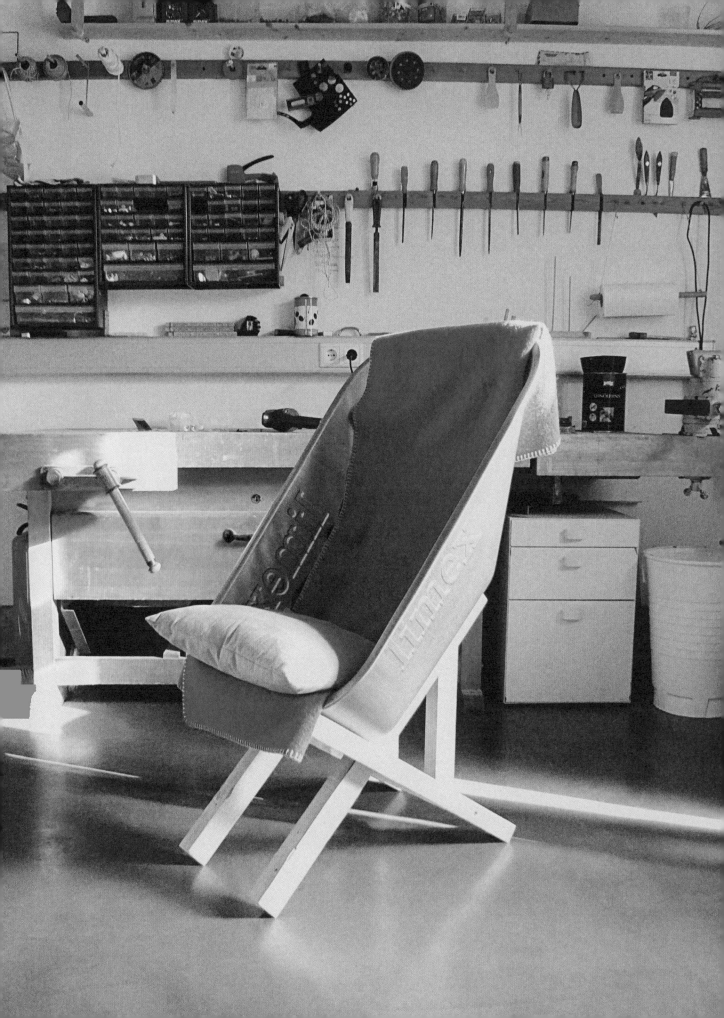

WHAT YOU NEED

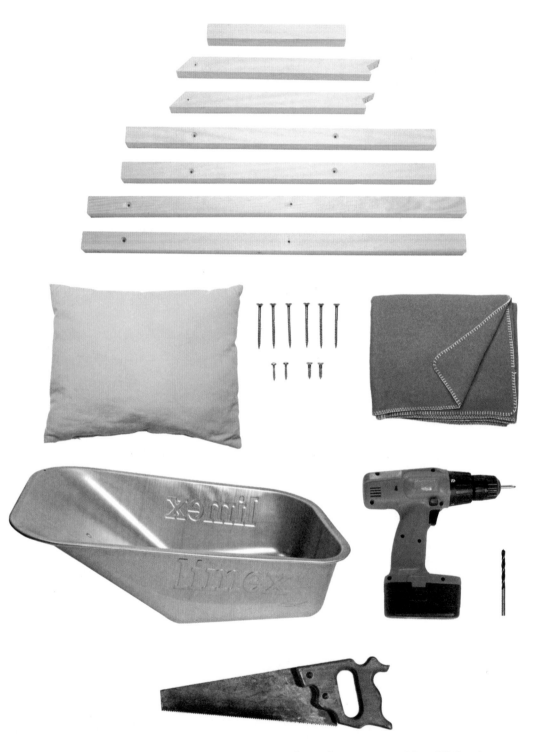

Wood strips cut to size: one piece 12 in (30 cm); two pieces 30 in (75.5 cm);
two 25 in (64 cm) and two 17 in (43.5 cm) long, these last cut at 45° angle
on one end, and with a right-angled notch cut out of the other end.
Pillow. Screws. Blanket. Wheelbarrow tub.
Drill and drill bit, ¼ in (6 mm). Saw.

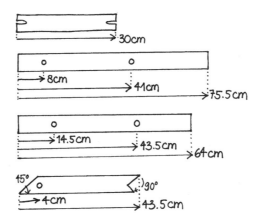

1. Bore holes in the wood strips as follows: 3 in (8 cm) and 16 in (41 cm) from the end of the 30 in (75.5 cm) strip; 6 in (14.5 cm) and 17 in (43.5 cm) from the end of the 25 in (64 cm) strip; 1½ in (4 cm) from the angled end of the 17 in (43.5 cm) strip.

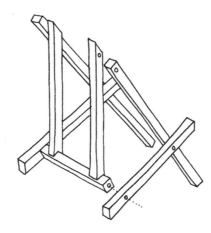

2. Screw the pieces together as shown.

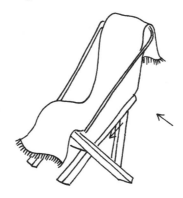

3. Bore four holes in the wheelbarrow tub where it is to lie against the back bars. Screw the tub on. Choose your blanket and cushions, pad out the tub, and relax.

COST
US$60/£40/€53

PENDANT LIGHT BY
Yves Béhar

TIME
90 Min

AMPLIFY

Traditional chandeliers are made of numerous lights and crystals, but Yves Béhar wanted to change this equation. His Amplify lamp, which he originally created for the Austrian glass company Swarovski, consists only of one crystal, one low-energy LED light, and a faceted paper shade. The result is beautiful reflections and rainbow color bursts – the expected effect of multiple crystals – made simply by amplifying the use of a single crystal. "It is a pursuit in our work to try to achieve the maximum effect with the minimum amount of materials and energy – designing consciously and conscientiously, while still maintaining an element of beauty." Of course you can use all kinds of glass diamonds, even colored ones, to customize your Amplify lamp.

Yves Béhar is a design entrepreneur – founder and CEO of fuseproject, an integrated design and branding firm, established in 1999. His humanitarian work includes One Laptop Per Child, which has given 2.5 million laptops to children in developing countries, and free corrective eyewear to schoolchildren in Mexico and California. Béhar has won more than two hundred awards, was named a Top 25 Visionary by *TIME* magazine, and was recently named "Most Influential Industrial Designer in the World" by *Forbes*.

WHAT YOU NEED

Thick, translucent paper stock. Cutter. Large ruler. Bulb socket, with
cord, plug, and fastening ring. Cardboard ring for attaching crystal.
LED bulb. Crystal. Flexible wire.

INSTRUCTIONS

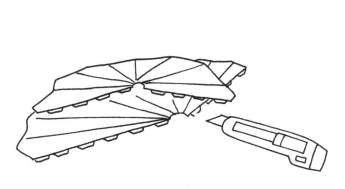
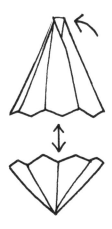

1. Scan pattern from page 213 and scale up 500 percent (5 times) to get the correct size, or download from phaidon.com/diy. Print onto heavy, translucent paper. Then cut and score along the template lines.

2. Begin assembling the halves of the lantern separately. Align the opposing edges and insert the tabs into their corresponding slots. Keep a few of the tabs on the top half open and then assemble the top and bottom halves together.

3. Place the cardboard ring on the threaded coupling and then screw on the fastening ring. Attach the wire and crystal by inserting the wire through the two holes on the crystal attachment ring. Adjust as needed to ensure that the crystal is hanging directly below the light.

4. Gently flex the top opening around the light and crystal fixture, and then close the final edge using the remaining tabs. Straighten and adjust the lantern as needed, and connect the cord to power.

COST
US$15/£10/€13

FABRIC PUPPET BY
Ai Weiwei

TIME
90 Min

CAONIMA

At first glance, these sock puppets seem like nothing more than kids' toys. But, as so often with the work of the Chinese conceptual artist Ai Weiwei, there's more to them than meets the eye. In 2009, the video of an innocuous children's song, showing grazing alpaca camels, went viral on YouTube in China. In China, the alpaca is *caonima*, and this is also a rather earthy and popular insult to the receiver's mother in Mandarin. Within days, the alpaca had turned into a way of symbolically flipping the bird to censorship of the Internet in China. This is a theme that Ai Weiwei has gratefully seized on ever since, as with his alpaca puppet for this book.

Ai Weiwei was born in Beijing and is viewed as the most important Chinese artist in the world today. His work covers varied disciplines — photography, installation, and sculpture — and it turns a critical eye on human rights abuses, exploitation, and pollution in his native land. Ai was also involved in the design of the national stadium in Beijing (the "Bird's Nest"). In 2012 he won the Václav Havel Prize for Creative Dissent. He lives freely in Beijing but is not allowed to travel abroad.

WHAT YOU NEED

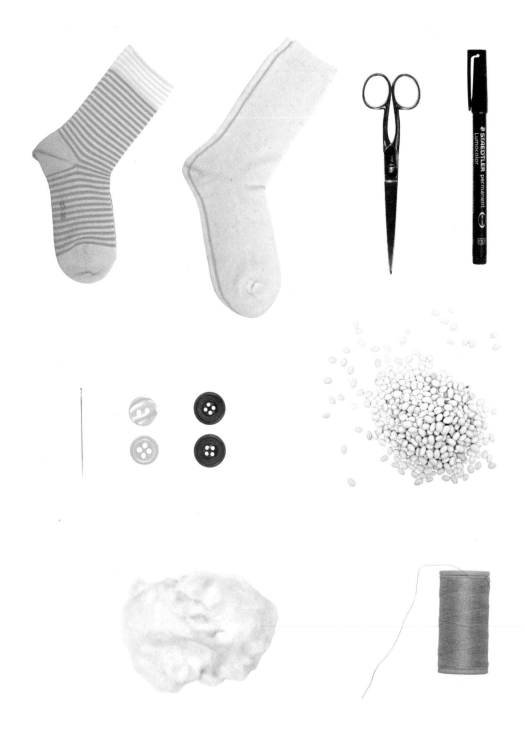

(Old) sock. Scissors. Marker.
Sewing needle. Buttons (for the eyes). Dried beans.
Wadding or cotton wool. Thread.

INSTRUCTIONS

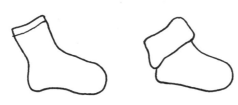
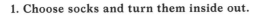

1. Choose socks and turn them inside out.

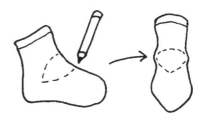

2. Use a marker to mark out the first area to stitch as shown.

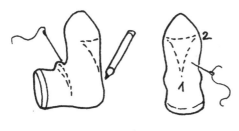

3. Stitch together at marks, so that the sock forms a right angle. Mark the second area on the sole and sew the marks together.

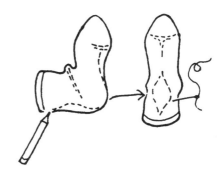

4. Mark the third area to stitch and sew closed.

5. Turn the sock right side out. First stuff it with wadding, and then weigh it down with beans.

6. Finish off with a layer of wadding, to prevent the beans from slipping, and sew the top closed.

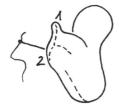

7. Sew the tail in two steps, from point 1 to point 2.

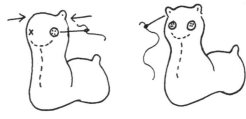

8. Mark eyes and attach buttons. Pull out two little ears over the eyes, and tie them with threads.

COST
US$35/£22/€30

COAT RACK BY
Sebastian Bergne

TIME
60 Min

COAT RACK

A bucket is a commodity whose shape is so completely determined by its function that it leaves little room for modification, which makes it all the more interesting when it is removed from its original purpose and becomes part of a design. "This coat rack is the result of careful improvisation rather than serious furniture design. I like the idea of putting a single recognizable object at the center of the piece but in an unexpected way. In this case: a plastic bucket. Its design, strength, and quality define the geometry and stability of the rack." It goes without saying that it's worth choosing this key component very carefully.

Sebastian Bergne was born in Tehran. He graduated from the Royal College of Art, London, and in 1990 founded his design studio there. His everyday products and furniture for companies such Authentics, Habitat, and Vitra have won numerous awards and are held in major museum collections. With his humanistic design approach, focused on essentials, Bergne pursues questions of cultural change, something that makes him a sought-after speaker and curator.

WHAT YOU NEED

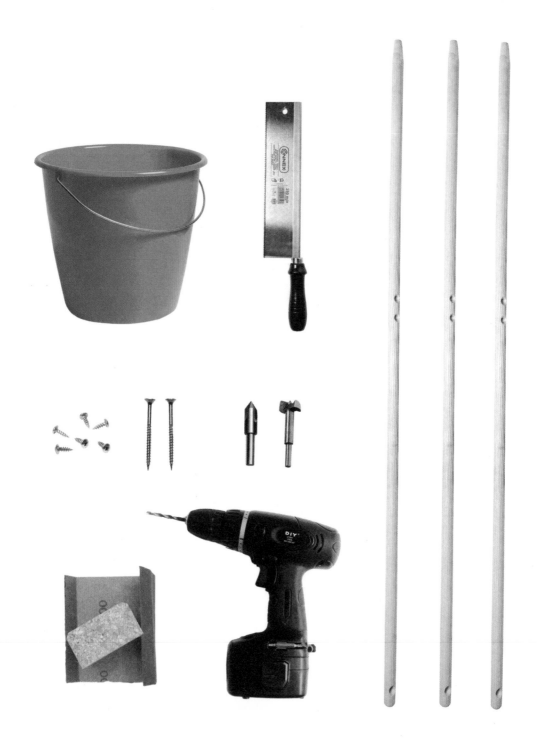

Strong plastic bucket. 3 wooden dowels, 65 in (165 cm) long × 1½ in (3.5 cm)
diameter. Saw. Sandpaper and block. 6 dome-headed wood screws.
2 wood screws. Drill/screwdriver. Drill bit, ¼ in (5–6 mm).
Countersink drill bit. 1½ in (3.6 cm) forstner bit.

INSTRUCTIONS

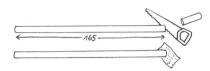

1. Take care to choose a strong bucket with tapered sides. Cut your dowels to 65 in (165 cm) long and round the ends using sandpaper or similar.

2. Drill roughly ¼ in (5–6 mm) holes through two of the dowels 16½ in (42 cm) from one end. Then follow this up with a deep countersink drill bit to hide the screw heads.

3. Mark out the hole centers on the top and sides of the bucket and then drill them using the ¼ in (5–6 mm) drill bit and 1½ in (3.6 cm) forstner bit.

4. Hold the ends of the dowels together temporarily using two or three strong rubber bands in the position of the screw holes.

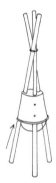

5. Slide the dowels through the holes in the top of the bucket, and slide the bucket up until the angle of the side of the bucket matches that of the dowels.

6. Screw in three dome-headed screws to hold the bucket in position. Check that the bucket is level. Then screw in the other three screws and tighten all.

7. When the bucket is in position, screw the remaining two screws into the tops of the dowels to lock the coat stand together.

8. Remove the rubber bands. Use coat stand.

COST

US$25/£16/€22

PENDANT LIGHT BY
Patricia Urquiola

TIME

360 Min

SNAP

True, this lamp requires a certain amount of patience. You need to set aside a good half a day at least, as you're going to have to cut up a lot of cardboard. The payoff: a lamp that will cast elegant patterns of light and shade on your wall. Patricia Urquiola explicitly encourages those who follow her design to experiment by using, for example, cardboard in two different colors: "That gives the lamp itself a playful look, and if you're lucky it will also produce chromatic light effects. It was important to me to design something that wouldn't cost a lot and could be made with things that can be found in every home."

Patricia Urquiola is one of the most versatile and successful furniture designers of the last few decades. She is Spanish, from Oviedo, and her studio in Milan has clients such as Moroso, B&B Italia, Foscarini, Driade, and De Padova. She has designed more than 250 pieces of furniture, many of them best-sellers such as the Smock armchair. She has been selected on several occasions as Designer of the Year by various institutions and magazines.

WHAT YOU NEED

Snap fastener punch and die. Protractor.
Light bulb, 5 in (12.5 cm). Cable and socket.
Strips of cardboard (cut to size).
Utility knife. Hammer. Hollow punches, ⅛ and ¼ in (4 and 7 mm)
diameter, or hole punch. 90 standard snap fasteners.

INSTRUCTIONS

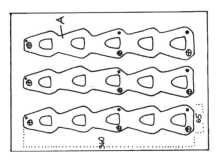

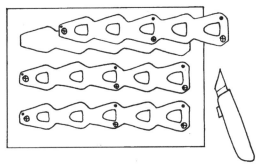

1. Copy the pattern from page 214, or download it from phaidon.com/diy. Cut the pieces for the lampshade (A) and make holes for the fasteners (C is for the upper parts, B for the lower parts of the fasteners), using the ⅛ and ¼ in (4 and 7 mm) punches.

2. Cut out the pieces cleanly with a cutter. In total, 30 pieces are required.

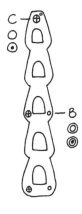

3. Attach the upper (C) and lower (B) parts of the fasteners at the places marked.

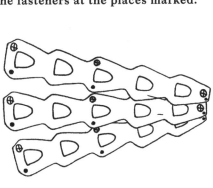

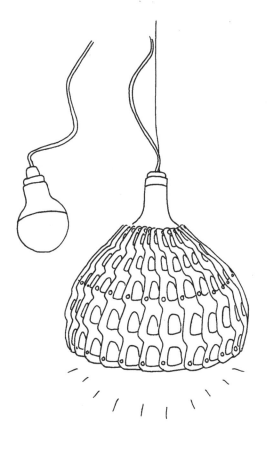

4. Connect all the pieces together with the fasteners to make a symmetrical lampshade.

5. Draw the cable and the bulb through the completed lampshade from beneath, until the shade lies loosely on the bulb.

COST

US$25/£16/€22

BENCH BY
Pauline Deltour

TIME

60 Min

SHOE MAN

This piece of furniture solves a common problem in hallways. Especially in family households or shared apartments, the hallway is often paved with a colorful heap of shoes. You have to pull them on while squatting on the ground, of course. The Shoe Man – its name an allusion to the famous Schuh Mann bar in Munich, where Deltour liked to go when she was working with Konstantin Grcic there – is a bench and shoe rack in one. Quickly cobbled together, its purist design means it fits into any interior and its dimensions can be scaled as desired. "I've always wanted to make a bench – and now I've made it serve two purposes."

Pauline Deltour was born in Landerneau, France. For her thesis at the University of Applied Arts in Paris, she developed a wastepaper basket out of steel wire that the head of Alessi liked so much that the label took over mass production. French-born Deltour spent three years working with Konstantin Grcic in Munich, and now she lives and works in Paris. Her designs for Muji, Alessi, Kvadrat, and others are characterized by precision and experimentation.

WHAT YOU NEED

Drill. Drill bit, ⅜ in (8 mm). Wood glue. Wood pegs, ⅜ in (8 mm) diameter.
Jigsaw. ¾ in (18 mm) thick wood boards, A: 41 × 10¼ × ¾ in (105 × 26 cm);
B: 40 × 3½ in (102 × 8.8 cm); C: 40 × 4 in (102 × 10 cm);
D(×2): 16½ × 8½ in (42.2 × 22 cm).

INSTRUCTIONS

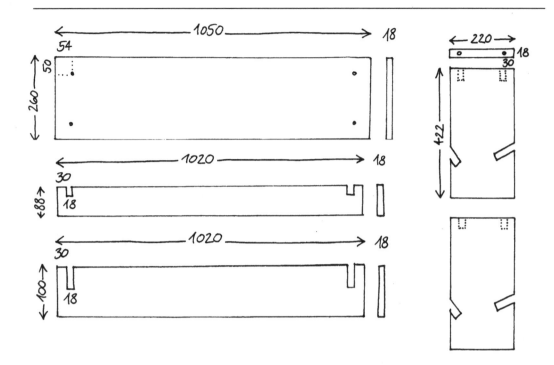

1. Cut the boards to size. Drill holes 2 in (50 mm) in from the corners on Board A. Saw ¾ in (18 mm) notches 1¼ in (30 mm) from each end of Boards B and C. Saw out oblique notches from the two Boards D following the pattern on page 216.

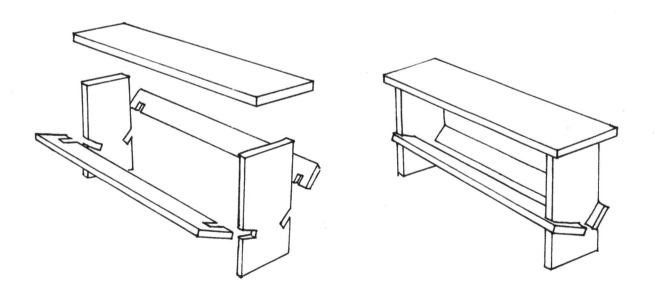

2. Sand down the edges. Apply glue to the contact surfaces, insert the wooden pegs, and fit the boards together.

113

ROPE RUG

The Autoban architecture and design practice is in Beyoğlu, the historic fishing and shipping district of Istanbul, and near the old markets where sailors and fishermen buy the things they need for everyday use. The idea of making a carpet from rolled-up rope came from this world. "The big ship tanks, the simple, natural materials on the markets, and the industrial ambiance are never-failing sources of inspiration for us. The Rope Rug consists of natural materials and contains no gluten or other toxic materials. You can unravel it at any time and use the rope for something else."

Autoban design studio was founded in Istanbul in 2003 by Seyhan Özdemir and Sefer Caglar. It now has more than thirty-five employees and has made an international name for itself with its innovative and experimental projects in the fields of interior design and product design. Autoban furnishes hotels, houses, restaurants, and airports and has its own international brand name. The studio has won several international architecture and design awards.

WHAT YOU NEED

Wood plate ¾ in (20 mm) thick, cut into a hexagon, 10 in (25 cm) wide.
Rope ¾ in (20 mm) thick, 60 yards (55 m) long for a carpet of around
47 in (120 cm) diameter. 3 pieces of heavy thread, each 60 in (153 cm) long.
Upholstery or saddler's needle, at least 6 in (15 cm) long.
Scissors. Staple gun. Staples.

INSTRUCTIONS

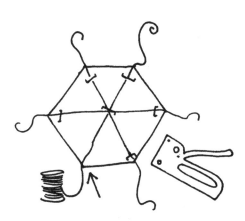

1. Staple three pieces of thread in a star shape on the underside of a precut wooden board, as shown, so that they stick out from the corners of the board. The ends should protrude the same length as the planned size of the carpet.

2. Thread one of the pieces of thread through the needle. Lay the rope against one corner of the wooden board. Stick the needle with the thread through the rope and pull so that the rope lies tightly against the wooden board.

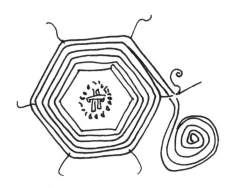

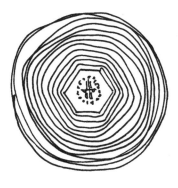

3. Roll the rope around the board and attach it at each corner with needle and thread.

4. If more or various ropes are used, you can tie them together with a simple knot.

COST
US$50/£33/€44

LAMP BY
Field Experiments

TIME
20 min

COUNTERWEIGHT LAMP

This lamp originated from a series of experiments carried out by the design collective Field Experiments in Indonesia and is based on one simple rock being the pivotal component of the structure. "Combining common materials and elements from the world is a staple process for generating new ideas," says Benjamin Bryant, cofounder of the collective. The lamp employs those materials for their inherent traits and is also a metaphor for the fragility of modern human beings and their fatal dependence on technology. "It makes one think just what would happen if the rock was removed."

Field Experiments is Benjamin Harrison Bryant, Karim Charlebois-Zariffa, and Paul Marcus Fuog – a nomadic design collective. From June to September 2013, Bryant, Fuog, and Charlebois-Zariffa set up a studio and home in Lodtunduh, Bali, a farming community situated on the outskirts of Ubud. They conducted daily experiments in stone masonry, woodcarving, batik, painting, basket weaving and kite making with a community of local craftspeople.

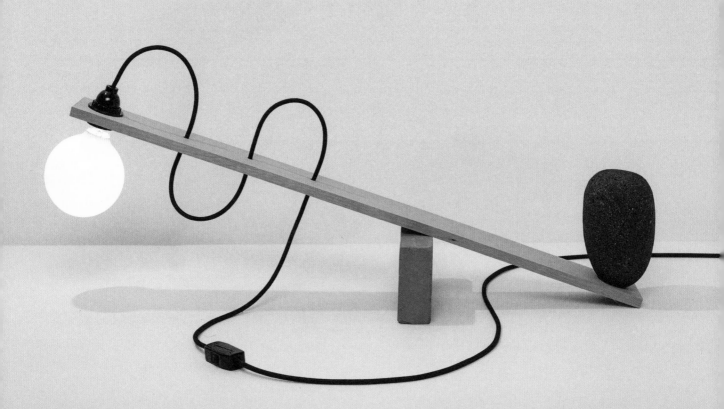

Piece of wood 36 × 4 × ½ in (91.5 × 10 × 1.25 cm). Large brick. Stone.
Power cord 16 ft (500 cm) long. White globe bulb.
Light bulb socket with shoulder. Plug.
³⁄₈ in drill bit. 1½ in hole saw or forstner bit. Drill.

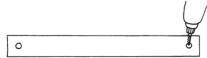

1. Find a roundish stone to serve as the counterweight. Cut your piece of wood to size.

2. Drill a hole at each end of the board: One for the socket, one for the rock rest, each about 1½ inches in diameter (depending on socket size).

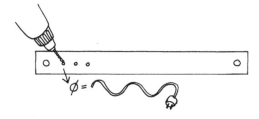

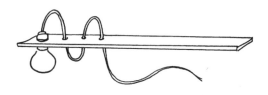

3. Drill three more small holes close to the socket hole, big enough for the power cord.

4. Attach the power cord to the bulb socket and weave it through the board. Attach the plug.

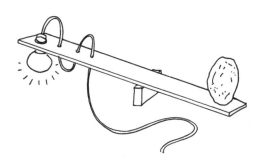

5. Prop up the board with the brick at about the midpoint, and set the stone counterweight. Screw the bulb into the socket, plug in, and turn on.

FLYING SHELF

This design, by the Swiss duo Kueng Caputo, is delightfully simple: The shelves consist of four wooden boards fitted together, a piece of rope, and two eye screws. It was exhibited in 2011, at the Designeast fair in Japan, as part of a do-it-yourself workshop. Various designers were invited to come up with a piece of chipboard furniture made from the ruins left by the tsunami. The money that came in from the sale of the plans was devoted to helping those affected by the earthquake. Flying Shelf is two things at once: A piece of DIY furniture for people who have lost everything, and a functional item for purists. "We like the fact that the product continues to develop without us. Every set of shelves will look different. Of course, instead of chipboard, you can use solid oak or MDF."

Sarah Kueng and Lovis Caputo live and work in Zürich. The two women are both Swiss and show their sometimes experimental, sometimes everyday designs throughout the world. Their Never Too Much series of leather furnishings garnered wide praise and was exhibited in both design fairs and art galleries. They prefer to work "at the boundary between product design, art, and interior design."

WHAT YOU NEED

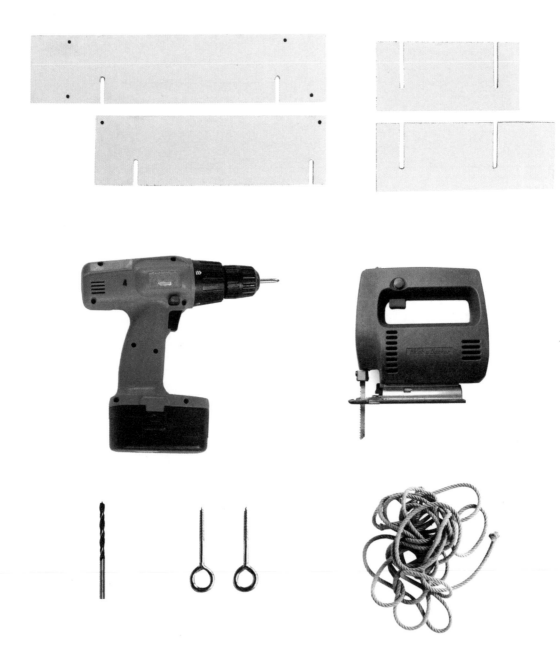

4 wooden boards, each 8 in (20 cm) wide × ½ in (1.25 cm) thick,
with these lengths: A: 17 in (43.5 cm); B: 21 in (54 cm);
C: 35 in (90 cm); D: 28 in (70 cm).
Drill. Jigsaw. Drill bit, ⅜ in (10 mm). 2 eye screws.
Rope, about 22 in (540 cm) long, ¼ in (7 mm) thick.

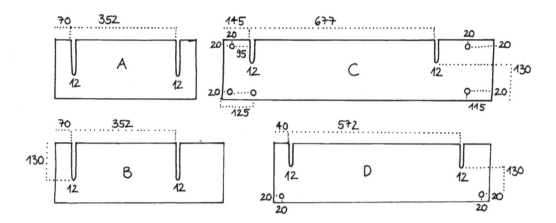

1. Cut slits ½ in (12 mm) wide, at 2¾ and 14 in (70 and 352 mm) from one end on A and B; at 5¾ and 26¾ in (145 and 677 mm) from end of C; and at 1½ and 23 in (40 and 572 mm) from end of D. Then bore ⅜ in (10 mm) holes in the corners of C and D, ¾ in (20 mm) from the ends. Or if you prefer, have it all made for you at the hardware store.

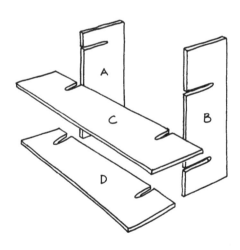

2. Fit the pieces together to make the shelf.

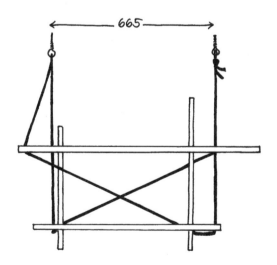

3. Insert hooks in the desired position on the ceiling, roughly 26 in (66.5 cm) apart. Pull the rope through the holes as shown, and knot. Hang up the shelf.

DRILL IT

The idea is as simple as it is enticing: You take any object, not too big, make a dime-sized hole in it, and you've got yourself a candleholder that's unique in the world. The possibilities are endless. "It means you can put things like unwanted birthday presents, rolling pins or statues you've got tired of, dull (thick) books, and other such items to new use," explains Maarten Baas. Is there any risk of it catching fire? He's even thought about that. The hole in Drill It is fitted with a suitable metal pipe in which the candle is placed. Still, the usual warning applies: Don't leave candles to burn unattended, and use at your own risk!

Maarten Baas was born in Arnsberg, Germany, and studied design in Eindhoven and Milan. He won fame for Smoke, a series of charred and varnished items of classic furniture based on the work of artists such as Gaudí, Eames, Rietveld, Sottsass, and the Campana Brothers: these pieces have been acquired by museums and private collectors. In 2005 he set up, together with Bas den Herder, a studio that is now responsible for producing Baas's individual pieces in small editions.

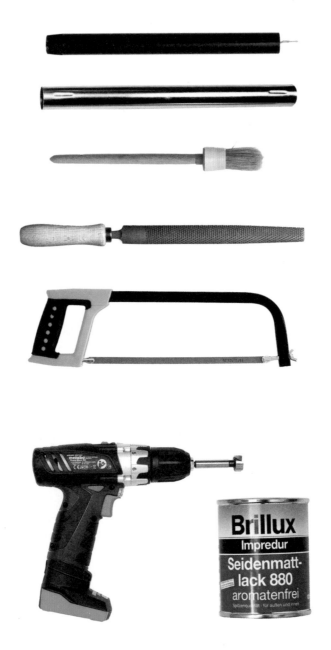

Candle. Metal pipe (same diameter as the candle).
Brush. File. Hacksaw. Drill.
Forstner bit (same diameter as the pipe). Varnish.

INSTRUCTIONS

1. Choose whatever objects you think will make good candleholders.

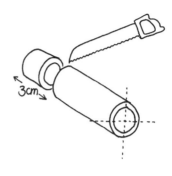

2. Saw off a piece of metal pipe approximately 1¼ in (30 mm) wide and smooth with a metal file.

3. Cut or drill hole(s) in the object. These should be the same diameter as the metal pipe.

4. Insert the piece of metal pipe into the object.

5. Varnish the object the same color as the candle.

6. Place the candle in the hole in the object. Light, but do not leave unattended while burning.

COST
US$60/£40/€53

FAN BY
Rodrigo Almeida

TIME
120 Min

WINDBOX

It took a long time for the fan to develop from its original shape to the electric desk fan we know now. It gives us comfort, but also represents our alienation from the things around us: the electric fan is a product that can be manufactured so cheaply that it's viewed as disposable. This is where Rodrigo Almeida comes in: "By taking a hand in the simple construction of a table fan and adding a handmade element to it, I'm going back along the historical path this object has traveled. When you make something for yourself, you forge an emotional connection with things. This is just what is missing these days."

Rodrigo Almeida was born in São Paulo and is one of the few autodidacts in the field of product design. He is always looking for influences from his own region and Brazilian culture. Almeida doesn't work for big producers, but singlehandedly and in small editions. His work is gaining increasing recognition at international exhibitions.

WHAT YOU NEED

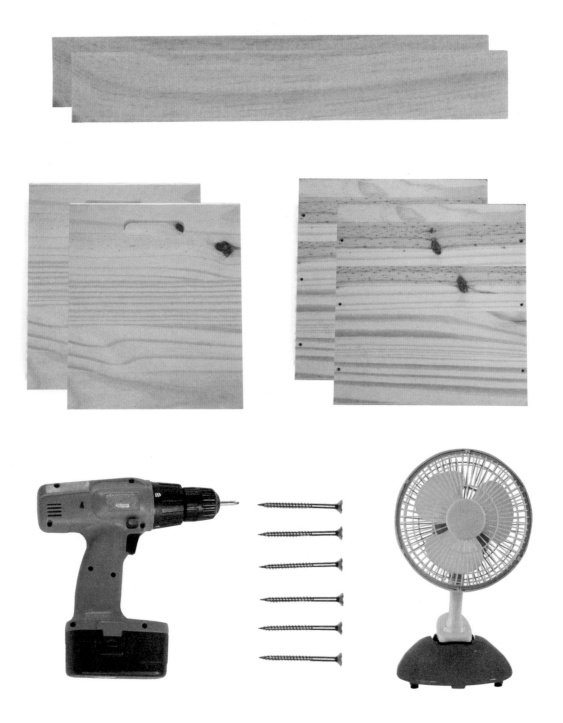

Wooden slats for feet.
Wood blanks for box. Drill.
Screws. Electric fan.

INSTRUCTIONS

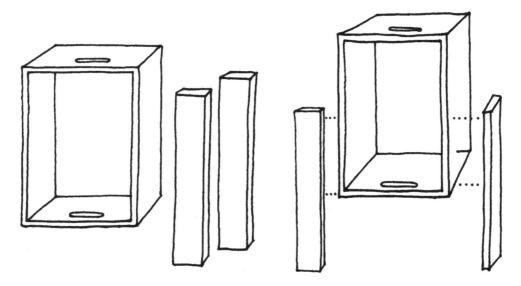

1. The wooden crate can be obtained ready-made, or else you can make it yourself. The size is determined by the fan. Paint the chest and the legs whatever color you want.

2. Attach the wooden slats to the crate as legs (either with glue, nails, or screws), one on the front and one on the side.

3. Attach the fan inside the box with screws or glue. Tip: Use a fan that already has a screw hole.

MAGPIE

"God is the best designer." And: "Nature is my greatest inspiration." A designer can't brandish these phrases to impress anyone these days, because with 3-D printers, virtually anything can be copied. The Italian design duo Formafantasma doesn't even try to copy God – they simply draw on the store of things that nature offers us. Thus, a shell becomes a saltcellar and a block of stone becomes a nutcracker, with the simple addition of a smooth wood base. "We use these objects on our tables at home. This requires no design. We've just turned the beautiful things we find to our own purposes – like thieving magpies."

Andrea Trimarchi and Simone Farresin make up the Italian design duo Formafantasma, based in Amsterdam. Thanks to their experimental, cross-border, design-based approach, they shot to stardom soon after completing their studies at Design Academy Eindhoven. Their designs from food residues, fish skins, and charcoal all challenge ingrained thought patterns. Their customers include Vitra, Lobmeyr, and Fendi.

Scallop shell. Oyster shell. Stone.
Wooden board. Drill and forstner bit 1¼ in (30 mm).
Sandpaper and block. Saw.

INSTRUCTIONS

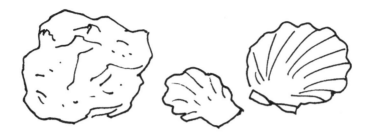

1. Find or buy a nice hand-sized stone, an oyster shell, and a scallop shell.

2. Cut two boards to approximately 8½ × 5½ × 1 in (21.5 × 14 × 2.5 cm) and sand the edges.

3. Drill a recess in the board with the forstner bit for the nuts. The stone will be used to crack them. Fill the scallop shell with sea salt and the oyster shell with pepper.

FLOWERPOT STAND

"Things that you make yourself need mainly to be functional and durable, like a set of shelves" – such is the view of Sam Hecht. "But I was curious to see whether it was possible to find a new aspect to a short-lived everyday item." Flowerpots are often viewed just as containers that should be covered over with decorative planters. We usually see them only from above. They stand on the floor or the windowsill. This design changes all that, since it raises the flowerpot to be level with our eyes. Three stakes use the tension created between the saucer and the flowerpot to keep the plant upright. The whole arrangement is a sculpture of plates, sticks, and plants that represents more than the sum of its parts.

Sam Hecht was born in London and studied industrial design at the Royal College of Art. He is one of the most important representatives of minimalist design. He has worked for, among others, the renowned architect David Chipperfield and the design studio IDEO. In 2002, together with the American designer Kim Colin, he founded Industrial Facility. Their clients include firms such as Whirlpool, LaCie, Magis, Yamaha, and the Japanese lifestyle department store Muji.

WHAT YOU NEED

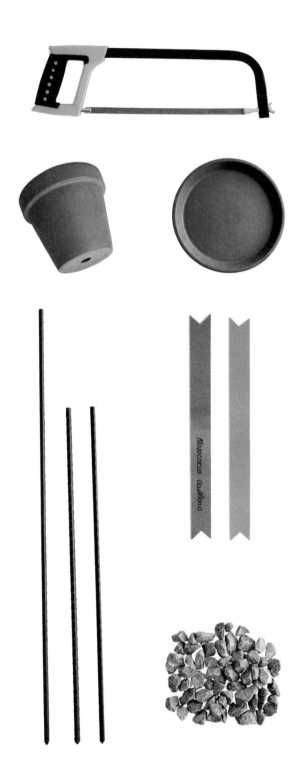

Hacksaw. Terracotta flowerpot, approximately 8 in (20 cm) diameter.
Terracotta saucer, approximately 20 in (50 cm) diameter.
Three metal plant supports. Flower label. Gravel.

INSTRUCTIONS

1. Mark out an equilateral triangle on the saucer. Insert the stakes through the hole in the base of the flowerpot, and fan them out on the plate so that the pot stands on them.

2. Mark two of the stakes even with the top of the flowerpot.

3. Take the stakes out of the flowerpot, and use a hacksaw to cut them off at the marks. Then, position again as in step 2.

4. Spread gravel around the stakes. Pot the plant in the flowerpot. Place the flower label on the end of the remaining long stake.

5. Water!

NEW PLANS 2005/2015

Jonathan Olivares originally designed New Plans for the Home in 2005, as a series of posters with full-scale diagrams that could be used to facilitate the installation of wall-mounted furniture for the home, using standard shelf brackets and lengths of wood. "DIY was something I engaged in as it presented a format, an opportunity to produce work at a time when I did not yet have clients. It was my first published work." For this book, one of the original designs has been re-proportioned and reworked so that its assembly instructions can be delivered in book form. "I like the idea of revisiting a project ten years later."

Jonathan Olivares was born in Boston and graduated from Pratt Institute. In 2006 he established his design office based in Los Angeles that works in the fields of industrial, space, and communication design. Olivares's work engages a legacy of form and technology, and asks to be used rather than observed. Among his clients are Knoll, Nike, and Danese Milano, and his work has received many design awards, including the Compasso d'Oro and the GOOD DESIGN Award.

WHAT YOU NEED

8 shelf brackets. Wood boards, 12 in (30 cm) wide × ½ or ¾ in (1.3 or 2 cm) thick, with the following lengths: top 37¾ in (96 cm) long; bottom 37¾ in (96 cm) minus the thickness of both sides; side slats 20⅜ in (52 cm) long. Screws for brackets. Screws for boards. Ruler and level. Pencil. Drill/driver. Saw.

INSTRUCTIONS

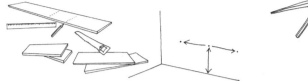 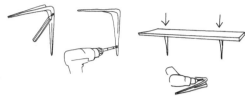

1. Measure the lengths of the four slats of wood needed to build the shelf. Mark lines and cut the wood. Measure 30 in (76 cm) from the ground to locate the bottom shelf.

2. Mark the bracket holes for the bottom slat with the level. Screw the bracket into the wall, and screw the shelf to the brackets. Make sure that the distances between the brackets and the ends of the shelf are equal.

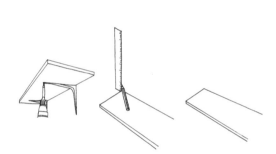 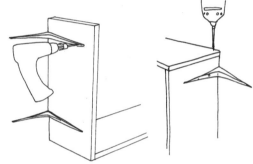

3. With the level, mark the placement of the side shelf and the brackets, which should be placed 3 in (7.5 cm) from the ends of the shelf. Repeat for both sides.

4. Using a ruler, mark points near the rear corners of the top shelf ⅜ in (9 mm) from the side and the rear of the slat. Place the upper shelf slat on the two side slats, and screw through the mark into the side slats.

5. Position the side slat of the shelf so that its bottom edge is flush with the bottom of the lower horizontal slat, and screw the brackets to the wood. Repeat for the left and right brackets.

COST
US$25/£16/€22

TEA COZY BY
Bernotat&Co

TIME
45 Min

APOLLO 11

Bernotat&Co became known for Chair Wear, a collection of "clothes" for old chairs. For this book, the two designers, Anke Bernotat and Jan Jacob Borstlap, took on an item that has fallen a little out of fashion, but whose usefulness is indisputable: the tea cozy. "It's seen as fuddy-duddy, as a throwback to tea parties in the 1950s. We wanted to change all that, and so we've given it a new interpretation, in the shape of a contemporary high-tech variant." Apollo 11 consists of thermal foil (also known as space blankets), which is used in first aid and for covering exhausted marathon runners so that they don't succumb to a chill after their run. "Tea will be safe, too, with our tea cozy."

After working for Norman Foster and Jasper Morrison, the German designer Anke Bernotat set up her own studio in Amsterdam in 2007 to create products for life, work, and public space. Her partner, the Dutch exhibition designer Jan Jacob Borstlap, joined the team in 2012. Her aim is to "recombine old, forgotten solutions with nowadays needs to create surprising and useful objects." Bernotat teaches industrial design in Essen.

WHAT YOU NEED

Sewing machine. Fabric tape ¾ in (20 mm) wide.
Space blanket. Gold- or silver-colored thread.
Double-sided tape (narrow). Re-positionable adhesive tape.
Tape measure. Pins. Scissors. Waterproof marker.

INSTRUCTIONS

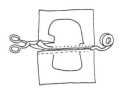

1. Copy or trace the pattern on page 218 and tape together, or download from phaidon.com and print.

2. Measure overall height (A), spout height (B), and circumference of the teapot.

3. If needed, adjust the cut-out pattern.

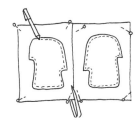

4. Spread out the space blanket, and fold along its short side (silver facing silver). Continue to fold until it measures approximately 12 × 32 in (30 × 80 cm).

5. Fix the foil with pins. Draw the cutting pattern with a waterproof marker, twice. Mark a second, dashed line approximately ¼ in (7 mm) within the first outline. Cut the foil through in the middle.

6. Sew the lower edges together on both halves, and cut out. With your hand between the two middle sections, turn inside out.

7. Mark horizontal sections about 1³⁄₈ in (3.5 cm) wide with the removable tape. Stitch the sections, then carefully take away the tape. Finish the lower edges with fabric tape.

8. Fold a loop out of the remaining foil and stick it together with the double-sided adhesive tape. It should be about 1½ (3 cm) long by ½ in (1.5 cm) wide once folded.

9. Lay the loop upside down at the top edge of one of the halves. Stitch the two sides together with the insides out.

10. Carefully turn right side out. Have a nice cup of tea.

COST
US$12/£8/€10

AIRPLANE BY
Jaime Hayon

TIME
20 Min

TYS VICO 1

Designing always means improvisation and DIY. Anyone who thinks this is a terrible insult to designers needs only to take a look around in design studios, where the predominant smell is of spray glue and sawdust, and a whole lot of experimenting is done with paper, cardboard, and wood before reaching the stage of fine-tuning the prototypes. So it's not just paternal love that leads a star designer such as Jaime Hayon to design a toy plane for his young sons: There's a child lurking in every designer. Hayon's project, based on a template, is so uncomplicated that kids should be able to assemble it themselves with minimal help from their parents.

Jaime Hayon was born in Madrid. From his first sketches, he explored the boundaries between art, decoration, and design. Already active on the skateboard and graffiti scene as a teenager, he started with shoes, toys, and bathrooms, and now also designs hotels and restaurants. In 2007, Hayon was named one of *TIME* magazine's 100 most important designers of our time. His clients include Magis, Swarovski, and Camper. He lives and works in London.

WHAT YOU NEED

1 piece foam core (3-4 mm thick).
Spray mount. Cutter.
Paper clips.

INSTRUCTIONS

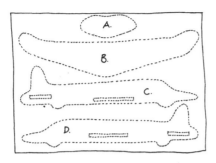

1. Photocopy the patterns on page 220, or download from phaidon.com. Cut parts A, B, and C from template, leaving some margin around the dotted line on each piece.

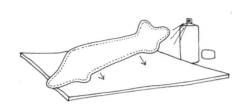

2. Use spray glue to attach the pieces to the foam core.

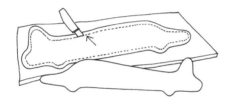

3. Use a cutter to cut carefully along the black dotted lines.

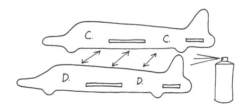

4. Cut out part D, and glue it to the opposite, blank side of part C.

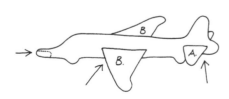

5. Insert part A through the hole labeled A, and part B through the hole labeled B.

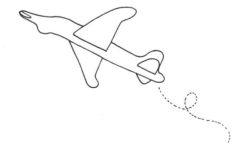

6. Attach a paper clip to the nose of the fuselage, using the gray dotted lines as a guide. Fly.

STANDING LAMPS BY
Ana Relvão &
Gerhardt Kellermann

LIGHTS A, B, C

A chair is a chair. But it can also be used as a clothes hanger or a stepladder. It is a favorite strategy of DIY culture to pry existing products away from their usual aims, as is the case with these lamps whose main element is a light reflector for professional photographers. You can find them in silver, gold, or white. For Ana Relvão and Gerhardt Kellermann, they formed the basis for a family of lamps. "It was important for us to keep everything as simple as possible; that's the only way you can ensure an idea stays open to other interpretations. A, B, C are our versions, but we'll be very happy if somebody tries a D, E, or F."

Ana Relvão and Gerhardt Kellermann live in Munich and share a design studio in Hechendorf, Germany, with Herbert H. Schultes, former head designer for Siemens and doyen of German industrial design. Relvão studied design in Portugal, where she grew up. Kellermann studied in Stuttgart. They are united by a desire to develop design solutions for every area of life, from the kitchen to the electric fan. Their clients include companies such as Bulthaup, Flötotto, and Auerberg.

WHAT YOU NEED

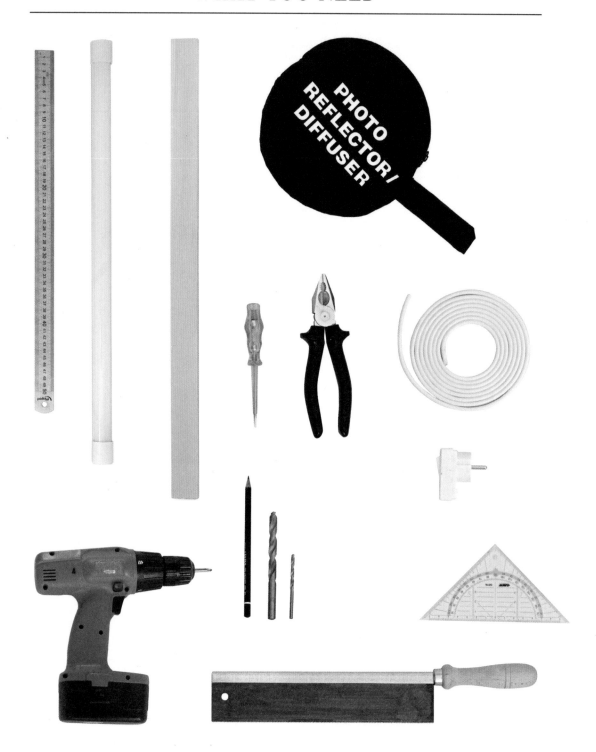

Ruler. 3 neon tubes with 24 in (60 cm) mount. Wooden slats, ¾ in (20 mm) thick.
A: 78 × 2 in (200 × 5 cm) and 20 × 2 in (50 × 5 cm); B: 45 × 2 in (114 × 5 mm);
C: 67 × 2 in (170 × 5 cm). Reflectors/diffusers in silver,
42 in (105 cm) diameter; gold, 36 in (95 cm); and white 32 in (81 cm).
Screwdriver. Pliers. 3 power cables, 8 ft (2.5 m) long, with plugs and switches.
Drill. Pencil. Drill bits. Screws. Protractor. Saw.

INSTRUCTIONS

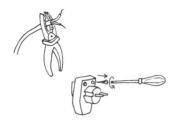

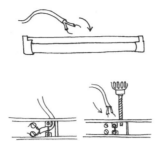

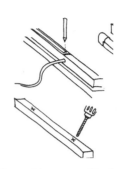

1. Strip the insulation from the cable end. Attach the other end to the plug.

2. Bore a hole into the side of the neon mount so that the cable will run through it. Attach the cable.

3. Place the mount flush to the end of the wood for lamps A and C; for lamp B, leave a gap of ½ in (12 mm). Mark the points for the holes and then drill.

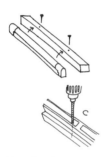

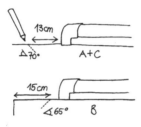

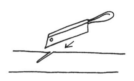

4. Fix the fitting to the wood, and insert the tubes. For lamp C, bore a hole all the way through the mount and wood so that it can later be attached to the wall.

5. For lamps A and C: draw a line on the wood at a 70° angle, 5 in (13 cm) below the neon tube mount. Repeat on the opposite side of the wood. For lamp B: draw a line at a 65° angle, 6 in (15 cm) from the top of the piece of wood.

6. Saw angled slits into the wood pieces where the marks are.

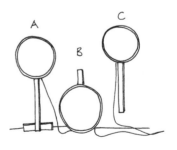

7. For lamp A, fasten the shorter piece of wood perpendicular to the end of the longer piece with two screws to form a base.

8. Fold the reflectors out and insert into the slits on the stands.

9. Lean against or mount on the wall and plug in.

COST
US$30/£19/€26

DESKTOP ORGANIZER BY
Benjamin Hubert

TIME
60 Min

FLEX

Anyone who's ever gone to a department store and tried to find a reasonable container for pens, scissors, or brushes that doesn't look faceless and utilitarian knows that the task is practically impossible. Benjamin Hubert's solution to this shortcoming is both elegant and easy to build: Small pieces of saddle leather are cut out following a set form, scored on the surface with a cutter, and curled. A household rubber band stabilizes the object. Thanks to the spiral structure, Flex provides room for short or long utensils. In addition, it is very suitable as a gift for mailing, when rolled out flat.

Benjamin Hubert was born in London. Since 2007 he has run his own studio, which is devoted to a material-driven and sustainable design approach. His designs for furniture, lighting, and interiors, including for Classicon, Moroso, and Ligne Roset, have received numerous prestigious awards, including the Red Dot Award and the iF Award. In 2010 he was named Young Designer of the Year by Elle Decoration International Design Awards.

WHAT YOU NEED

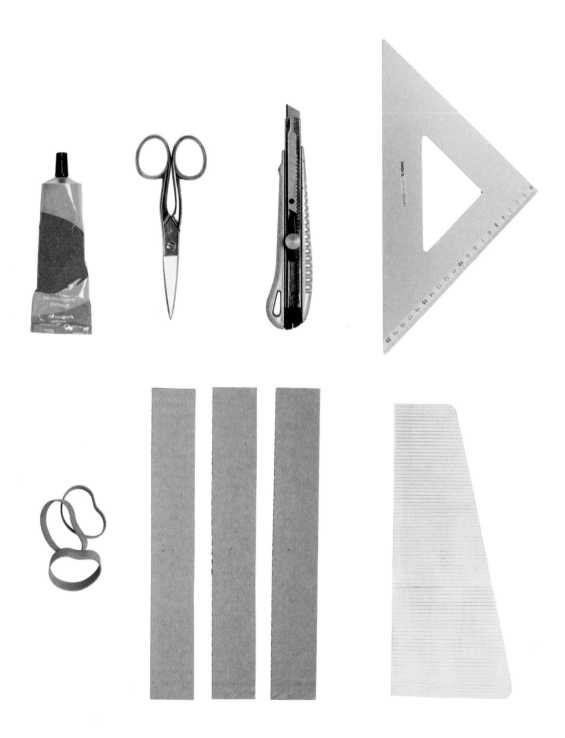

Glue. Scissors. Cutter. Set square.
Wide rubber bands, about 2¾ in (70mm) diameter. 23 strips of cardboard.
3 saddle leather pieces, 23¼, 16, and 11¾ in (590, 410, and 290 mm) long,
by about 7 in (178 mm) wide.

INSTRUCTIONS

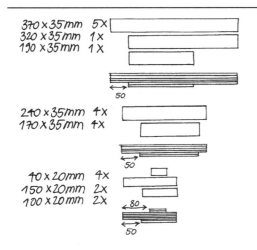

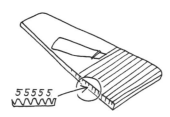

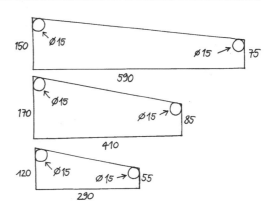

1. Cut the cardboard: Five pieces 14½ in (370 mm), one 12½ in (320 mm), and one 7½ in (190 mm), each 1½ in (35 mm) wide; four pieces 9½ in (240 mm) and four 6¾ in (170 mm), each 1½ in wide; Four pieces 1½ in (40 mm), two 6 in (150 mm), and two 4 in (100 mm), each ¾ in (20 mm) wide.

2. Cut the leather pieces. A: 6–3 × 23 in (150–75 × 590 mm); B: 7–3½ in × 16 in (170–85 × 410 mm); C: 4¾–2 × 11½ in (120–55 × 290 mm). Round the top corners with scissors.

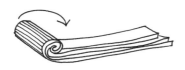

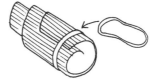

3. With the cutter and set square, score the leather every ¼ in (5 mm). Be careful not to cut all the way through the leather.

4. Glue the cardboard strips together according to the stacked side views in step 1.

5. When the glue has dried, roll up the leather (on the bottom) together with the cardboard (on the top). Fix the resulting roll with the rubber band.

COST
US$180/£120/€160

COATRACK BY
Sarah Illenberger

TIME
360 Min

JACKSTRAWS

The basic idea behind this coat rack is a classic game of jackstraws, or pick-up sticks. "I like the way you just need to change the size (approximate scale of 1:10) to produce something absurd," says Sarah Illenberger. It's very simple to construct: Purchase some wooden rods from the hardware store and sharpen them at the end; then use a stovepipe connection to fix them together in the middle. You cut rectangles out of different colored leather remnants, sew them down the long side, and pull them over the wooden pieces. The result is a piece of furniture that's not only very practical, but also a real eye-catcher. It's also a great coat rack for kids – you just change the size again (1:6).

Sarah Illenberger was born in Munich and studied at, among other places, Saint Martin's College in London. She lives in Berlin, where, in 2007, she set up her studio for illustration and visual concepts. Her clients include magazines from all around the world, photographers, and advertisers. Her work has won several design and graphics awards. In 2010 and 2011, she taught as a visiting professor at the University of Arts in Berlin.

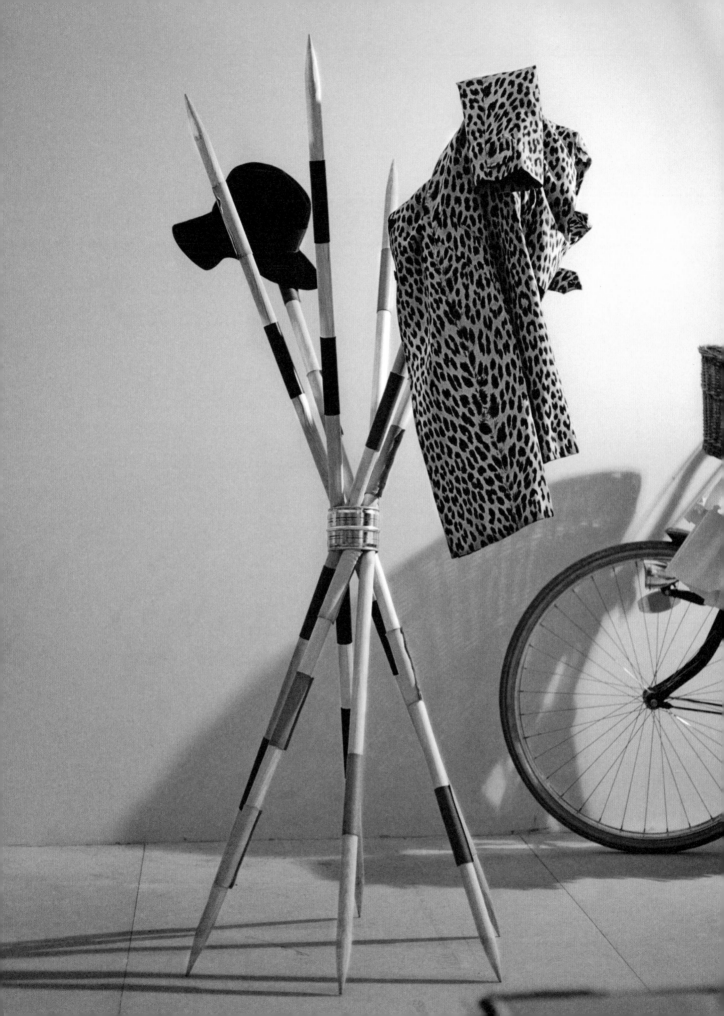

WHAT YOU NEED

Coarse and fine grit sandpaper. Wood file. Heavy thread.
Leather remnants, 4 × 6 in (10 × 15 cm).
6 wooden poles 1 in (2.5 cm) diameter, 5½ ft (170 cm) long.
Sewing needle. Stovepipe connection, 4 in (10 cm) diameter. Scissors.

INSTRUCTIONS

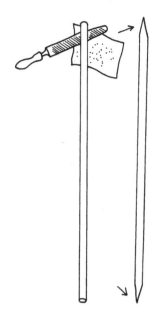

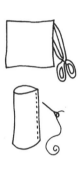

1. Sharpen the ends of the wooden poles with a wood file, and then with sandpaper.

2. Cut out the leather pieces and sew them together with thread of a suitable color.

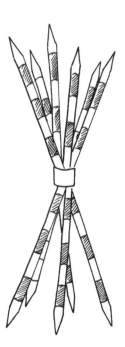

3. Pull the leather pieces onto the wooden stakes.

4. Push the stakes through a stove-pipe connection, and splay out at the top and bottom.

COST
US$1/£1/€1

SPATULA BY
Michael Marriott

TIME
20 Min

COFFEE SPATULA

Problem solving is one of the basic tasks of the designer. The good news is that problems never go away. The idea for these little kitchen helpers came to Michael Marriott as he was brewing coffee with his Alessi espresso machine, designed by Richard Sapper. The espresso tastes excellent, but the filter is difficult to clean. "I needed some kind of spatula, preferably made of wood, so as not to scratch the filter. I found a leftover piece of walnut, sawed and filed it into shape, and drilled a hole in it for hanging. I like tools whose purity is based on pure functionality." The basic principle of this spatula can, of course, be applied to any other espresso machine.

Michael Marriott was born in London. He is considered one of the most influential British designers of his generation. His furniture and household products for manufacturers such as Established & Sons, SCP, and Möve are characterized mainly by practicality, innovation, and fidelity to the materials. Marriott, who graduated from the Royal College of Art in 1993, won the 1999 Jerwood Furniture Award and has also made his mark as a curator of exhibitions.

WHAT YOU NEED

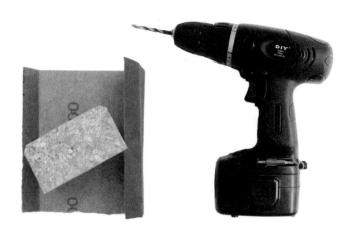

Wood scrap. Saw. Wood file.
Sandpaper. Drill. Drill bit, ¼ in (6 mm).

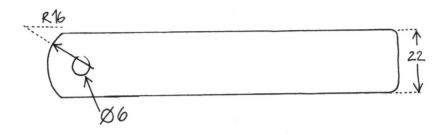

1. Cut the wood to 5 in long, almost 1 in wide, and about ⅛ in thick (125 mm long, 22 mm wide, and 3 mm thick).

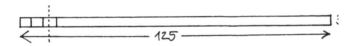

2. Mark a center point about ½ in (12–15 mm) from one end. Mark a ½ in (12–15 mm) radius across the end. Drill a ¼ in (6 mm) hole through center mark.

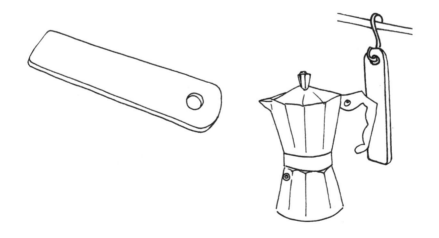

3. Sand all edges soft, with about 1/16 in (2 mm) radii at the corners.

COST

US$45/£30/€40

CHAIR BY
**Christophe
de la Fontaine**

TIME

120 Min

RENAISSANCE

"Germany is the land of hardware stores," says Christophe de la Fontaine. He drew inspiration from all the many things that can be found in these stores for his project – plastic buckets and tubs, for example. He uses them as the starting point for some very original garden chairs: "I wanted to put a well-established mass-produced article into a new context. The simple wooden construction for the legs means the result is a 'pièce unique.'" You can choose the type of chair you make by deciding for yourself on the kind of bucket and its color, as well as the size you cut it to. The same idea, of course, can also be applied to a whole family of ready-made chairs.

Christophe de la Fontaine initially studied sculpture in Luxembourg, then industrial design in Stuttgart. He was head of Patricia Urquiola's Milan design office from 2002 until 2010, when he founded his own studio. His clients include Moroso and Formagenda. For Rosenthal, he designed the much-lauded Format service. In 2012, together with his wife Aylin Langreuter, he founded the design label Dante – Goods and Bads. They live and work in Neukirche, in the Bavarian Forest.

WHAT YOU NEED

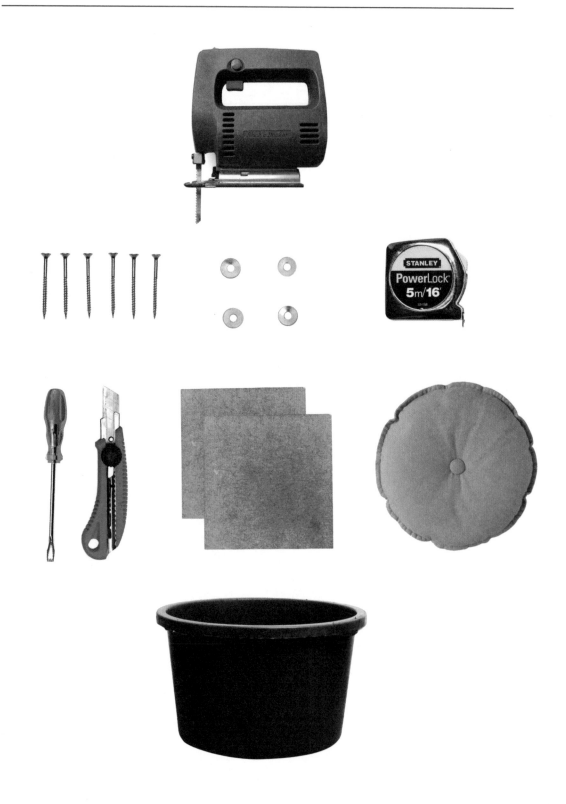

Jigsaw. Wood screws. Washers. Tape measure.
Screwdriver. Cutter. Wood panels. Seat cushion.
Plastic barrel (e.g., rain barrel, plant tub).

INSTRUCTIONS

1. Select a tub. For an adult chair, the diameter should be no smaller than 13 in (33 cm).

2. Cut the seat out using a carpet cutter, or similar tool. The type of shape you go for will depend on the size of the tub and the height of the seat, for example: armchair: 15 in (38 cm); easy chair: 16½ in (42 cm); standard chair: 18 in (45 cm).

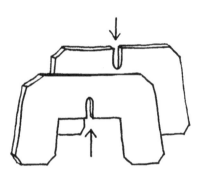

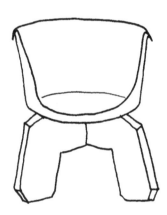

3. Cut out two wooden boards, ¾ in (20 mm) thick minumum, as shown, or get someone to do this for you. The two leg pieces are connected simply by a slit, which is exactly as wide as the wood's thickness. The height is defined as half of the distance to be connected. One leg piece has a slit at the top, the other at the bottom. The legs should be ¾ in (20 mm) smaller overall at the top than the diameter of the pail, and 4 in (100 mm) bigger overall at the bottom than the diameter of the pail, so that the chair will stand up without wobbling.

4. Bore holes through the pail and the legs, and screw the pail onto the legs with washers. If desired, varnish the legs. Pad out with suitable cushions, or sew together a suitable cushion yourself, with fabric and foam.

173

COST
US$15/£10/€13

SCULPTURE BY
Hella Jongerius

TIME
120 Min

PENGUIN

The idea for her "props" came to Hella Jongerius as she was looking at the impersonal home accessories with which artificial living spaces are equipped at furniture exhibitions. "I wanted to fill those interchangeable accessories with life, with poetry." She first exhibited her cardboard animals and fantasy creatures in 2007, at the Milan Furniture Fair. Here she shows you how to make a penguin from her acclaimed Props collection. You need cardboard, masking tape, and a certain amount of skill. Jongerius encourages people copying her designs to give their penguins their own individual shapes, varying them or painting them.

Hella Jongerius studied as a cabinetmaker before moving to Design Academy Eindhoven. In 1993, she founded her own firm called Jongeriuslab, and she opened a second branch in Berlin in 2008. She works for firms such as Maharam, Vitra, Makkum, and IKEA, and is known for the way she strives to bring craft and technology ever closer together. Her study My Soft Office, on the future of work, was exhibited at, among other places, the Museum of Modern Art in New York.

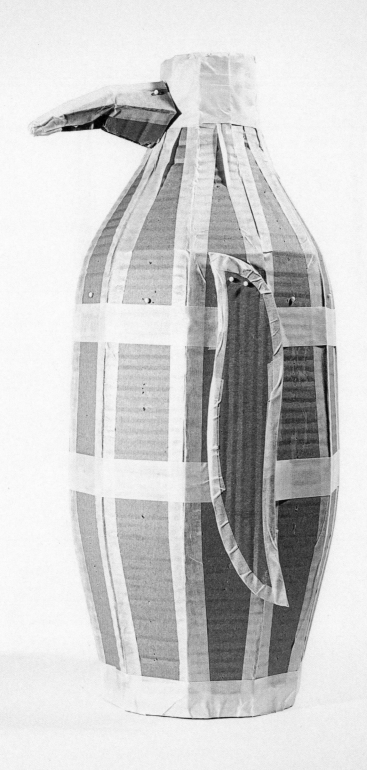

WHAT YOU NEED

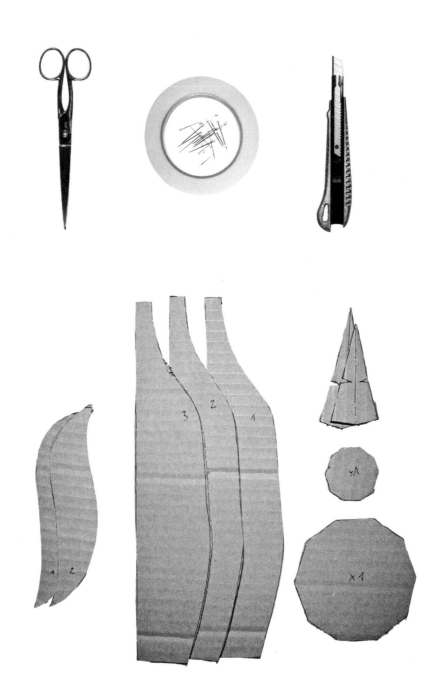

Scissors.
Masking tape and pins.
Cutter. Cardboard.

INSTRUCTIONS

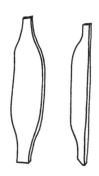

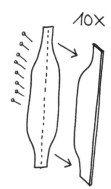

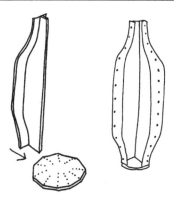

1. For the torso, draw a pattern (roughly the shape shown) on cardboard and cut out two models. You can choose your own size.

2. Cut one of the torso pieces in half vertically. Copy both halves 10 times over on cardboard and cut them out.

3. Stick the pieces together with pins. Glue to a ten-sided base also cut out of cardboard, or fix with pins.

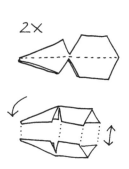

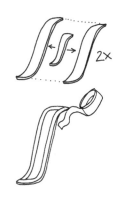

4. Connect and fix the torso with masking tape, horizontally and vertically.

5. Make four equally sized wings plus two smaller ones to sandwich between them. Tape up.

6. Attach the wings to the torso with pins.

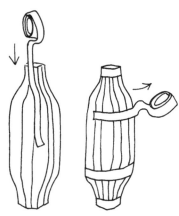

7. Cut out two pieces for the beak, fold, and join together with tape.

8. Attach the beak to the penguin's head with pins.

9. Paint in whatever colors you prefer.

COST

USD$45/£30/€40

SIDETABLE BY

Ana Kraš

TIME

90 Min

BOOK

When folding tables were invented, any aesthetic consideration was often neglected just to save room. But this side table proves that easy-to-stow furniture doesn't have to be disappointing to look at, and is indeed easy to make for yourself. Book isn't just an appealing way of displaying books and magazines; it can also readily hold coffee and cake and, when necessary, be folded away in a matter of seconds. Book can be made out of different materials (wood, cardboard) and painted in whatever colors you choose.

Since graduating from the University of Applied Arts in Belgrade in 2008, the young Serb Ana Kraš has worked as a furniture designer, photographer, and, on occasion, as a model. Her most successful projects include the pretty Bonbon Lamps, elegant pieces that she makes individually by hand. She lives and works in New York.

WHAT YOU NEED

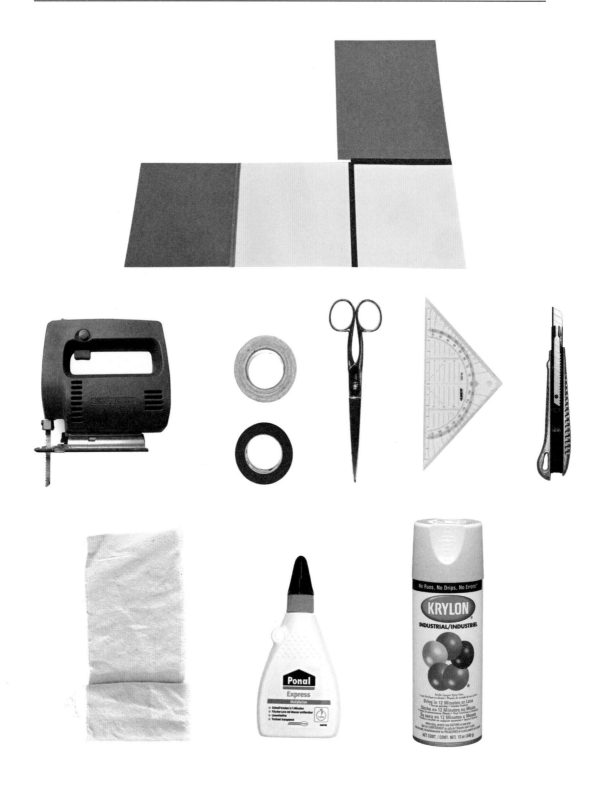

4 boards (wood or cardboard).
Jigsaw. Colored duct tape. Scissors. Protractor. Cutter.
Muslin. Wood glue. Spray paint.

INSTRUCTIONS

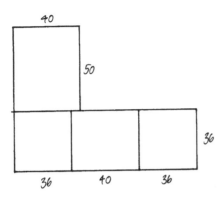

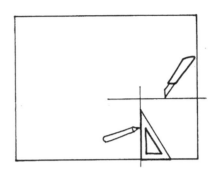

1. Decide on the size you want your side table to be. This one is 14 in (36 cm) high, with the three sides 14 in (36 cm), 14 in (36 cm), and 16 in (40 cm) long. The top is 16×20 in (40×50 cm).

2. Cut or saw the surface areas out, depending on the material. If necessary, sand down the edges.

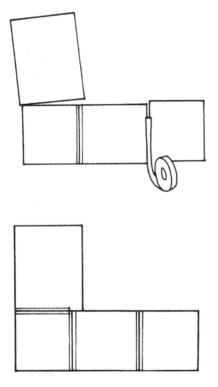

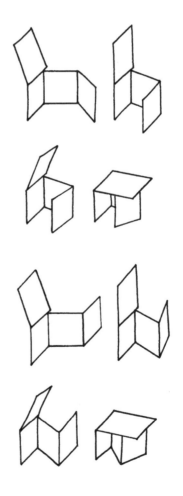

3. If using cardboard panels, connect with duct tape. For wooden boards, join with muslin and glue, and then with tape. Pay attention to the distance between the surfaces. It must be at least twice as wide as the thickness of the surfaces.

4. Set up the table so that it doesn't wobble. Decorate with paint, wallpaper, and so on as desired.

COST
US$115/£75/€100

SHELF BY
Matteo Thun

TIME
240 Min

BOOK LADDER

Alpine life is a recurring theme in the work of the designer and architect Matteo Thun, who was born in Bolzano, South Tyrol. His Book Ladder is a tribute to the bread ladder, a piece of furniture used by the Alpine people called the Walser, who store their fresh-baked rye bread loaves on it. The Walser were miners who left the Upper Wallis in the Middle Ages and spread across the Alps. Their furniture was free from any rustic decoration and remains timeless, as Thun's purist interpretation demonstrates: From square dowels, round wooden rods, and brass screws, he has created a simple, versatile shelf for storing and hanging personal items, books, and magazines.

Matteo Thun is an Italian architect and designer. He is a pioneer of ecological construction. His award-winning designs, both purist and iconic, follow the motto "Eco, not Ego." After working as a cofounder of the Memphis design movement, a lecturer at the University of Applied Arts in Vienna, and art director at Swatch, Thun founded his own company, Matteo Thun & Partners in 2001.

WHAT YOU NEED

4 long square dowels, 47 × 1¼ × 1¼ in (120 × 3 × 3 cm). 2 square dowels,
13 × 1¼ × 1¼ in (34 × 3 × 3 cm). 2 square dowels, 11 × 1¼ × 1¼ in (28 × 3 × 3 cm).
28 round dowels, 18 in long × about ½ - ¾ in (45 cm long × 14 mm).
Handsaw. Drill. Forstner bit, same diameter as round dowels.
Screwdriver. 8 long wood screws. 56 brass screws. Felt pads.

INSTRUCTIONS

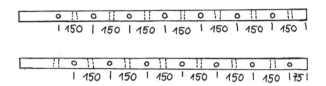

1. Drill seven holes in each of the long square dowels, 6 in (150 mm) apart, starting 6 in (150 mm) from the top. Then turn the dowels and drill seven holes in the other direction, but starting 3 in (75 mm) down from the top.

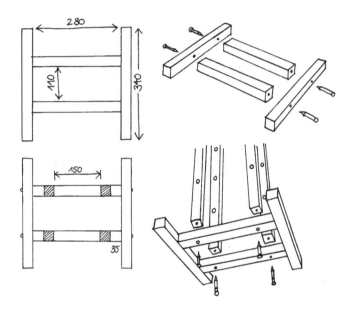

2. First screw the foot of the shelf together, then screw the four square dowels onto the foot using the wood screws.

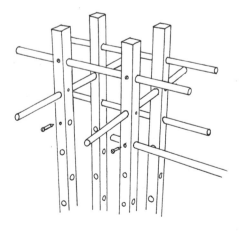

3. Fit the round dowels through the square dowels symmetrically, and fix with the brass screws.

COST
US$30/£10/€20

HOOKS BY
**Yvonne Fehling
& Jennie Peiz**

TIME
90 Min

SWIMMERS

Anyone with children knows that toys, especially the little plastic ones, are exciting for a while, but then eke out a miserable existence in some drawer in the kids' room. Yvonne Fehling and Jennie Peiz have rescued them from this fate and given them a new purpose: They can be used as clothes hooks. For this, admittedly, you have to remove the heads or saw them in half, but the kids will understand. And little creatures emerging from the wall create magical clothes hooks that look like something out of a Harry Potter movie.

Yvonne Fehling and Jennie Peiz both graduated from the Karlsruhe University of Arts and Design. Since 2006 they have run the design label Kraud, designing tables, chairs, lamps, and other accessories for the home. Their Stuhlhockerbank or "chair-stool-bench" (2007) won them acclaim. They describe their philosophy in these terms: "Craftsman-like finesse and an acceptance of contrasts." They live and work in Munich and Karlsruhe.

WHAT YOU NEED

Animal figures. Spray paint, white.
4 hanger bolts, 1¼ in (30 mm) long. Bolt anchors. Sandpaper.
Drill. Drill bit, ⅛ in (3 mm). Saw.

INSTRUCTIONS

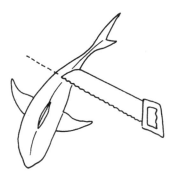

1. Saw a "hook" from a toy animal.

2. Rub down and polish with sandpaper.

3. Paint it whatever color you like.

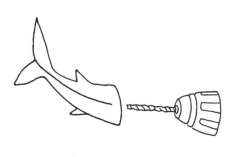

4. Bore a hole in the toy.

5. Screw hanger bolt into the hook.

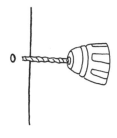

6. Bore a hole in the wall.

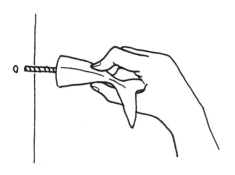

7. Screw in the hook.

STATION WAGON

If you have children, you'll know that playing isn't limited to just one place. This means that you don't just tidy up their stuff in one place: You have to do it here, there, and everywhere. With this project, Steffen Kehrle has tackled this problem and come up with a brilliant idea: the Station Wagon, a toy and mobile storage compartment in one. With one small gesture, the lid becomes a windshield, and the storage box itself turns into a toy. The car can be painted whatever color you, or your kids, like best.

Steffen Kehrle's designs often reveal their richness only when you take a second look at them. His motto is, "It's not hard to make things beautiful, and it's even easier to make things clever." After working with Ross Lovegrove at BMW and with Stefan Diez, Kehrle founded his own design workshop in Munich in 2009. In his furniture, exhibition ideas, and products, Kehrle plays with expectations and uses humor and improvisation to create style.

WHAT YOU NEED

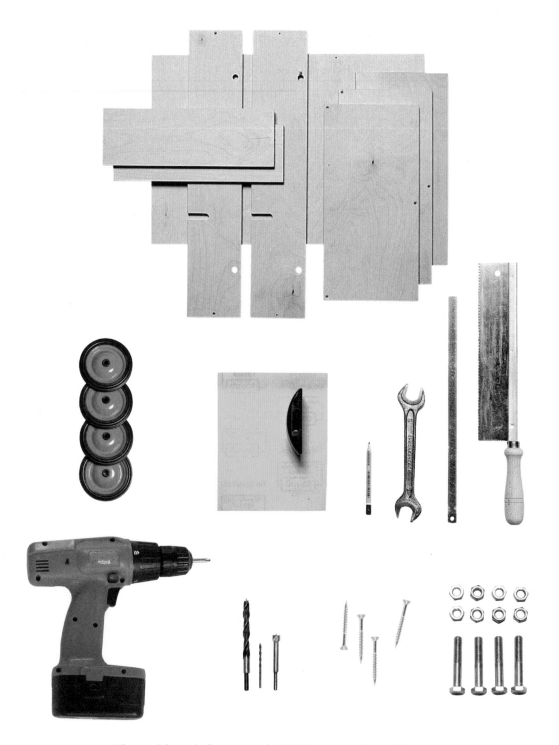

Plywood boards (cut to size). SPAX screws, 1½ in (36 mm).
Wheelbarrow wheels, 6 in (15 cm) diameter.
Sandpaper and block. Pencil. Wrench. Ruler. Saw.
Drill. Drill bits, ½ in (12 mm), ¹⁄₁₆ in (3 mm), and phillips head.
Hex screws and nuts, M12, 70 mm.

INSTRUCTIONS

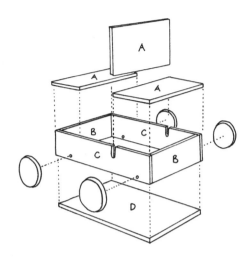

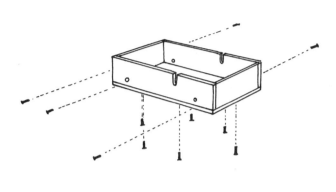

1. Download the plan with the measurements of A, B, C, and D from the phaidon.com page for this book. Cut out the pieces.

2. Screw together the side and base pieces B, C, and D with SPAX screws. Drill holes for the wheels.

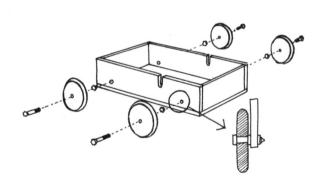

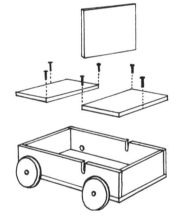

3. Mount the wheels with the hex screws and nuts.

4. Screw together the trunk lid and engine hood with SPAX screws.

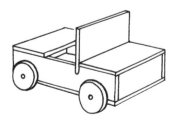

5. Fill 'er up, and drive off!

COST
US$50/£33/€44

PENDANT LIGHT BY
Ionna Vautrin

TIME
60 Min

PIÈCE MONTÉE

You can make absolutely everything out of Styrofoam: for example, a light with an elegance of line that conceals the beautiful simplicity of its construction. This lampshade consists of Styrofoam rings of varying sizes held together by fabric tape, both of which can be bought at any craft store. The shape of this pendant light, inspired by a French wedding cake called a *pièce montée* can be varied depending on how many and what sort of rings are used. Thanks to the semi-transparent Styrofoam, the light is pleasantly muted and warm.

Ionna Vautrin's lamps, which always look somewhat like small, glowing creatures, have made her a name to reckon with in recent years. She has designed them for firms such as Foscarini and Moustache. In 2011, she was given the Grand Prix de la Création of the City of Paris, and in the same year she set up her own workshop. Her brand is distinguished by organic shapes that communicate warmth and joie de vivre.

WHAT YOU NEED

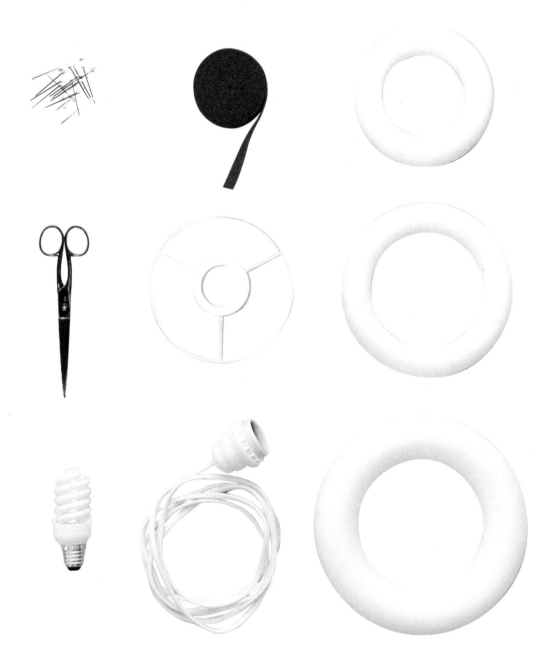

Pins. Ribbon. Styrofoam rings.
Scissors. Lampshade ring.
Energy-saving bulb. Cable and socket.

INSTRUCTIONS

1. Pin three pieces of ribbon to the lowest ring.

2. Attach the second ring to the lowest ring with three pieces of ribbon, alternating with positions of tape on the lower ring.

3. Place a new ring on top.

4. Place the lampshade ring between the last two rings.

5. Attach the third ring, aligning the fabric tape with the tape on the lowest ring.

6. Now attach ring 4 to ring 3 following the diagram for tape placement.

7. Tie ring 5 to ring 4.

8. Tie ring 6 to ring 5.

9. Tie ring 7 to ring 6.

10. Tie ring 8 to ring 7.

11. Tie ring 9 to ring 8.

12. Finish off and attach the cable and bulb socket.

COST
US$20/£13/€17

MAGAGINE BY
Maurizio Cattelan &
Paola Manfrin

TIME
45 Min

PERMANENT FOOD

Becoming a publisher and having your own glossy magazine can be easily done at home, according to the Italian artist Maurizio Cattelan. For his project, just grab a stack of magazines and start the skimming process. To get a better result, invite a bunch of friends to do the same. Rip out your favorite pages and carry out your own act of appropriation. Reassemble the pages and bind them in a second-generation magazine that says whatever you want it to say. "You can sell it, browse it, touch it, leave it open on the table. Once you get tired of it, feel free to throw it away. Others may use your waste as the beginning of a third-generation magazine."

Maurizio Cattelan is an Italian artist, born in Padua. He started his career making wooden furniture in the 1980s, and is now well known for his satirical sculptures. His work has been exhibited at many leading museums, including the Museum of Modern Art in New York and the Tate in London. The appropriated magazine project *Permanent Food* has been conceived and realized since 1995 by Maurizio Cattelan, Dominique Gonzalez-Foerster, and Paola Manfrin. To learn more about the history of the magazine, visit permanentfood.tumblr.com

WHAT YOU NEED

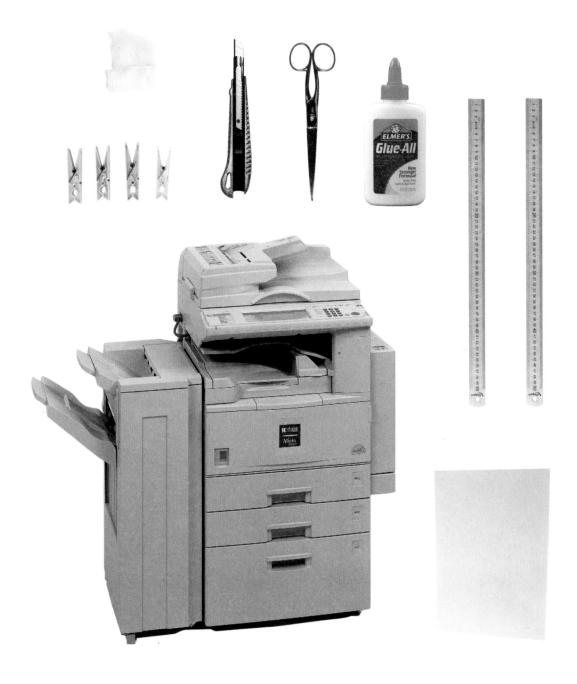

Magazines. Gauze strip. Four clothespins. Cutter. Scissors. Glue.
Two rulers. Photocopier. Cardstock.

INSTRUCTIONS

1. Collect some magazines with the same page size.

2. Select and rip out 192 pages.

3. Align the pages on the long side and glue the spine with paper glue.

4. Put the gauze strip on the glued part.

5. Press the spine with two rulers and four clothes pins and allow to dry.

6. Photocopy (scale to size) and cut out the two *Permanent Food* logos from page 222.

7. Choose an image for the cover and glue both logos on it, one across the top and one vertically along the left side.

8. Photocopy the cover with the pasted logos onto a piece of cardstock.

9. Glue the spine covered with the gauze strip to the inner side of the card cover with spine logo on it.

10. Fold and allow to dry.

COST
US$35/£22/€30

CHAIR BY
Piet Hein Eek

TIME
240 Min

EDAM CHAIR

Originally, this chair was designed for a community center in Edam, Holland, but it never went into mass production. It brings together all the characteristics that distinguish Piet Hein Eek's design philosophy: old-fashioned quality, sustainability, and craftsmanship. The chair consists of untreated matured-wood pieces – Eek's favorite material and his trademark. "There was practically no budget for this project, so we looked for pieces of wood from demolition sites. A shipbuilder and several volunteers helped us. So Edam turned into a collective DIY project." It's suitable as a piece of garden furniture or as a deliberately disruptive presence among classic designer chairs. A word of warning: Not for the uninitiated!

Piet Hein Eek studied at the Design Academy Eindhoven at the beginning of the 1990s, where his graduation pieces included bookshelves and chests of drawers in matured wood. He has stayed faithful to this idea up to the present day. These days, hundreds of employees work at his factory in Eindhoven. He sells his award-winning tables, beds, chairs and lamps in his own store and internationally through selected design galleries.

WHAT YOU NEED

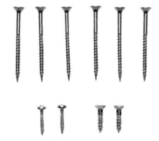

Screws. Reclaimed wood slats. Wood glue.
Cordless screwdriver. Jigsaw.

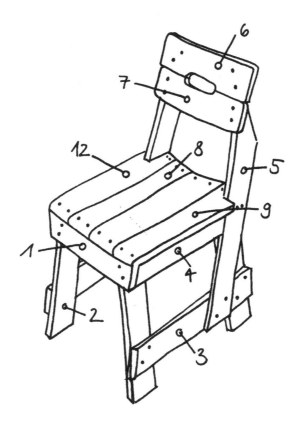

1. Download the plan with necessary pieces and dimensions from phaidon.com/diy. Cut out the pieces (or get someone else to do it). Nail or screw them together as shown and glue, if required.

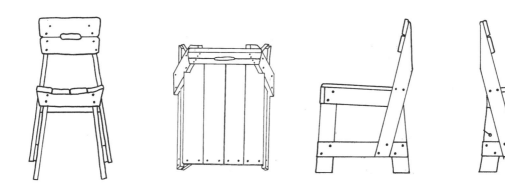

Edam chair – front view, from above, and from the sides.

COST
US$30/£19/€26

BIKE BAG BY
Werner Aisslinger

TIME
45 Min

BIKE BAG

Werner Aisslinger's idea pays tribute to the urban bicycle renaissance and to the low-budget culture of Berlin, where he lives. "I'd just bought myself a bike and needed to think about how I was going to transport my stuff around with me." Saddle bags were too bourgeois, and a rack or basket too impractical. The most elegant solution, he decided, would be a bag over the crossbar, as on Swiss Army bikes. He chose as his material the checkered fabric or plastic mesh bags that can be found anywhere, as they're cheap, solid, and weatherproof. "I wanted a quick and easy solution to an everyday problem that everybody's familiar with."

Werner Aisslinger was born in Nördlingen, Germany and, after working in Milan and Karlsruhe, he ended up in Berlin, where he runs a successful design office, Studio Aisslinger. His designs straddle the division between design, architecture, and art: his Loftcube, for example, is a 39-square-meter living space that can be flown by helicopter to anywhere in the world. His work can be seen in the Museum of Modern Art in New York, among other places.

WHAT YOU NEED

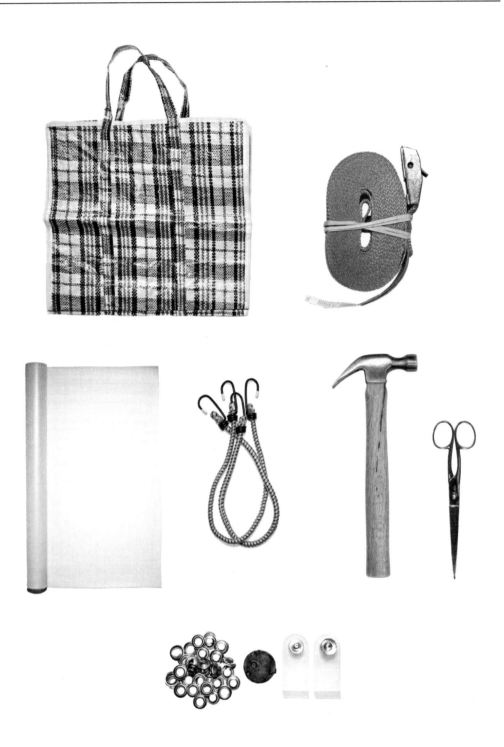

2 checkered fabric bags (with zipper). Set of lashing straps.
PVC lattice film, transparent. 2 bungee cords. Hammer. Scissors.
Set of rivets.

1. Fold the sides of the bag outward at the level of the zipper.

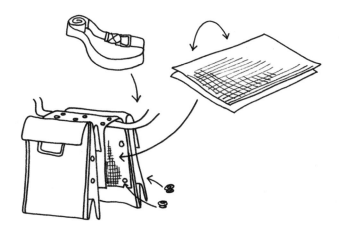

2. Using the rivets, attach both bags to the PVC film so that they can be hung over the crossbar of the bike (the lashing straps can be used as a hanging belt).

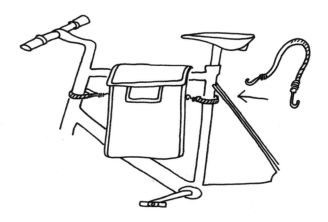

3. The bag can, if required, be fixed to the bicycle frame with bungee cords.

PATTERNS

PATTERN
Faye Toogood – TAPESTRY p.26

1. Separate ropes into groups of four and create Knot 1 eleven times across the top of the tapestry.

2. Next, using Knot 1 again, knot diagonally down from each side, shifting one rope inward with each knot until you reach the center two ropes.

3. Connect the two central ropes with the tape connection illustrated.

4. Use the two central ropes to create Knot 2 three times on each side – that is, with the three centermost ropes on each side.

5. Repeat the same knot on the same three ropes, going back toward the center.

6. Switch direction again and tie the same knot out toward the side, ten times on each side.

7. Connect the two new center ropes with tape, and use them to begin knotting Knot 2 out and in, in rows of ten.

8. After five rows of knots, connect the new center ropes with tape, and use them to knot Knot 2 out three times and back three times toward the center.

9. Now take the eleventh rope from the left and use Knot 2 to knot diagonally down and out toward the sides. Repeat on the right side.

10. Repeat the same knots on both sides down and inward ten times to create a triangular shape.

11. With the four center ropes, knot Knot 1 seven times straight downward. The rope will start to twist by itself.

12. Use tape to wrap 4 in (10 cm) of each of the outermost ropes, and 1 in (2.5 cm) of the eleventh rope from each side.

13. With the first rope on the left, knot Knot 1 diagonally down toward the center, knotting all but those in the central twisting column, then turn and knot six down and toward the side. Repeat on the other side of the tapestry.

14. With the new central rope (outside the twisting column), knot a row of five directly below and parallel to the previous. Take the new central rope and knot a row of four. Continue knotting from the center and reducing by one until you have a row of just one. Repeat on the other side.

15. Enjoy your tapestry!

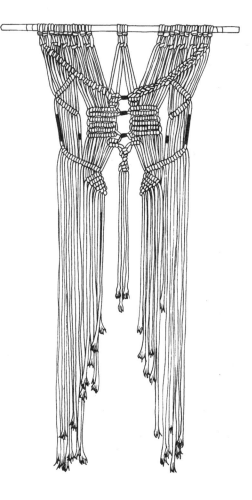

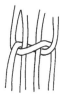

Knot 1   Knot 2

Taping

PATTERN
Yves Béhar – AMPLIFY p.94

Scan this template from the book and scale
up 500 percent (5 times) to get to the correct
size, or download 1:1 from phaidon.com/diy.
Copy onto thick, translucent paper and then
cut and score along the template lines.

213

PATTERN
Patricia Urquiola – SNAP p.106

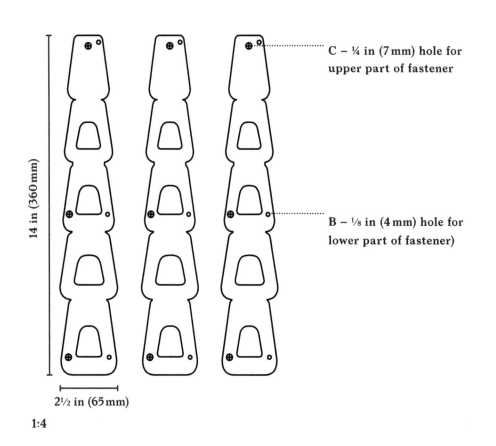

14 in (360 mm)

C – ¼ in (7 mm) hole for
upper part of fastener

B – ⅛ in (4 mm) hole for
lower part of fastener)

2½ in (65 mm)

1:4

1:1

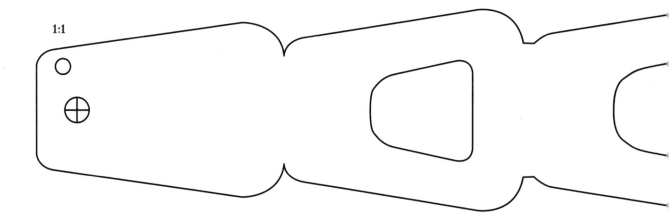

For Patricia Urquiola's Snap, 30 cut-out cardboard pieces are needed. Photocopy the large
pattern (1:1) onto a piece of 11×17 in or A3
paper, cut it out cleanly with a cutter, and
transfer it to thin cardboard. Three elements
fit onto one piece of 11×17 or A3. The holes
for the rivets are to be punched out beforehand,
with two sizes of hollow punch. Then the elements must be cleanly cut out with a cutter.
You can also find a printable version of this
1:1 pattern on phaidon.com/diy.

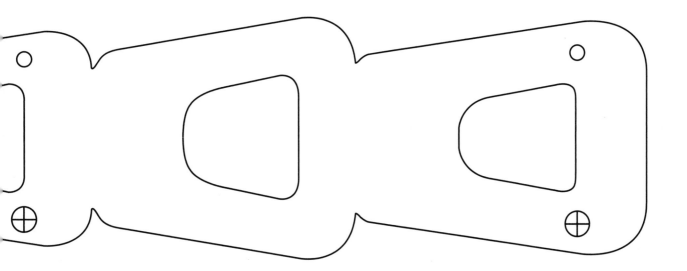

PATTERN
Pauline Deltour – SHOE MAN p.110

Photocopy this pattern 1:1, or download
and print it from phaidon.com/diy. Place
it against the boards that will form the
legs of the bench and transfer the pattern.
This will give the correct size and
position of the slots.

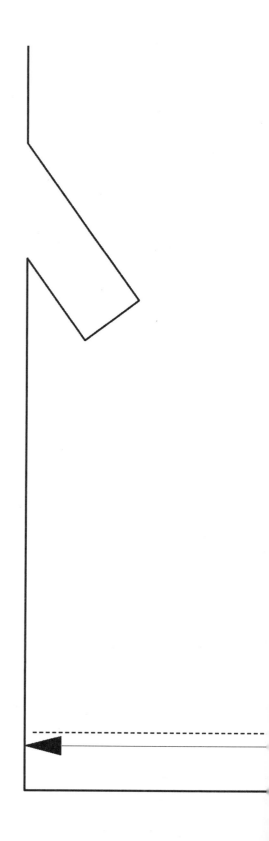

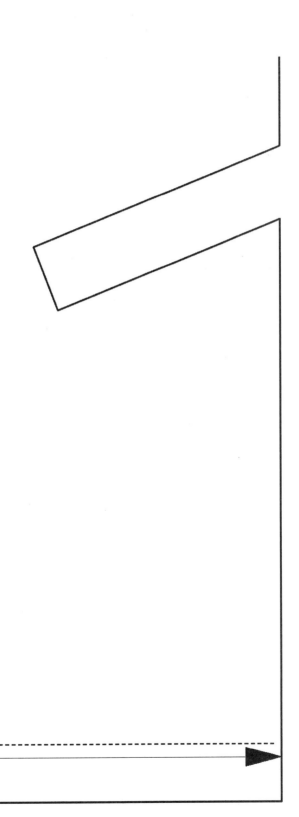

8½ in (22 cm)

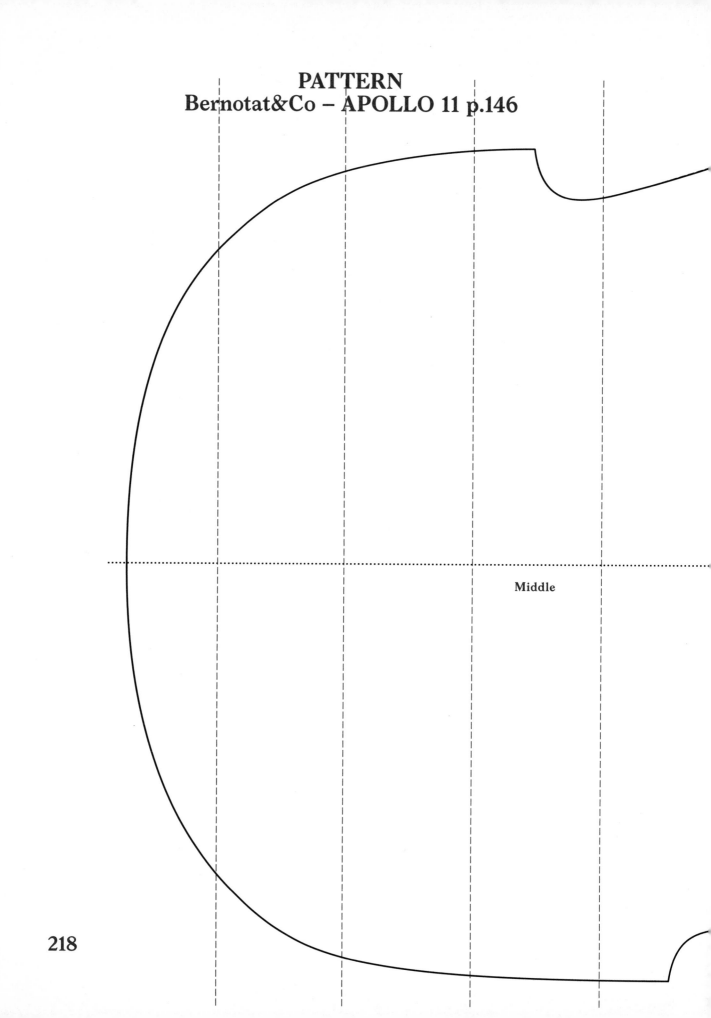

PATTERN
Bernotat&Co – APOLLO 11 p.146

Middle

218

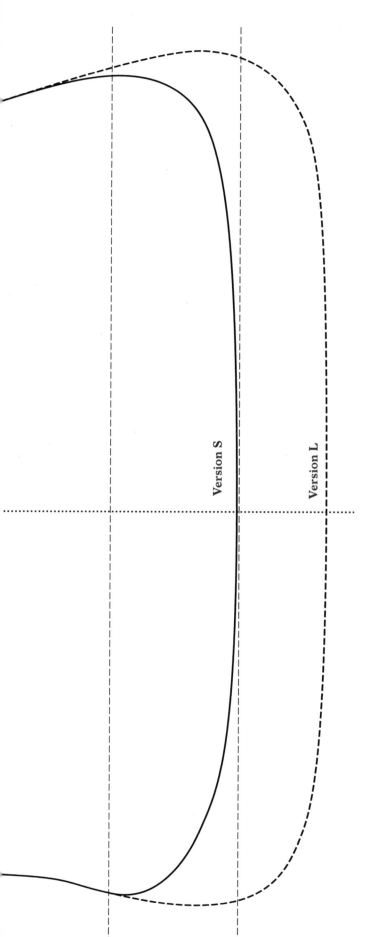

The pattern for the Apollo 11 tea cozy by Bernotat & Co. comes in two sizes. For smaller pots, Version S is recommended, and for medium to large sizes, Version L. Of course, you can also scale or vary the size if your pot doesn't fit either of these sizes. You can also find this 1:1 pattern in a printable version at phaidon.com/diy.

Version S

Version L

PATTERN
Jaime Hayon – TYS VICO 1 p.150

Copy this pattern 1:1 on a color copy
machine, or download from phaidon.com/
diy and print in colour. Carefully cut out
all pieces, leaving some white margin
around, before mounting on foam.

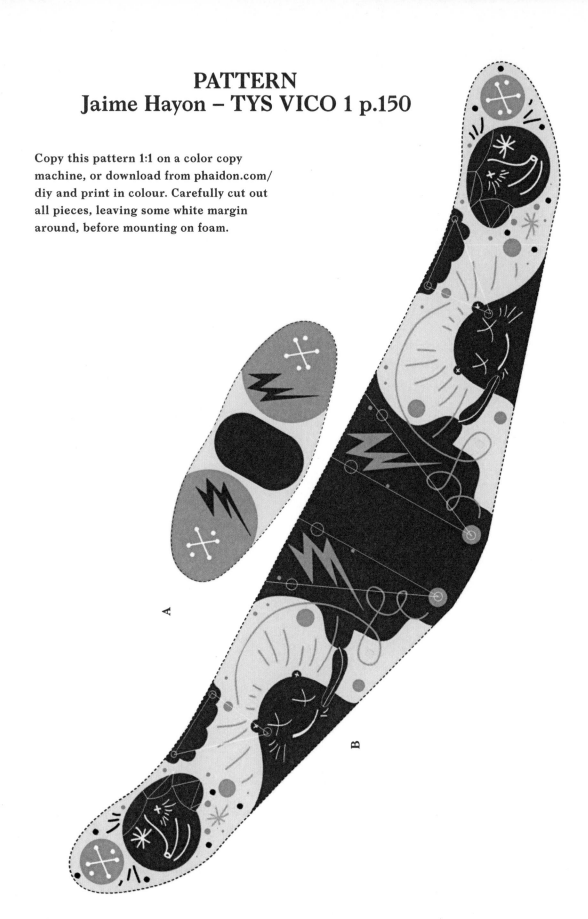

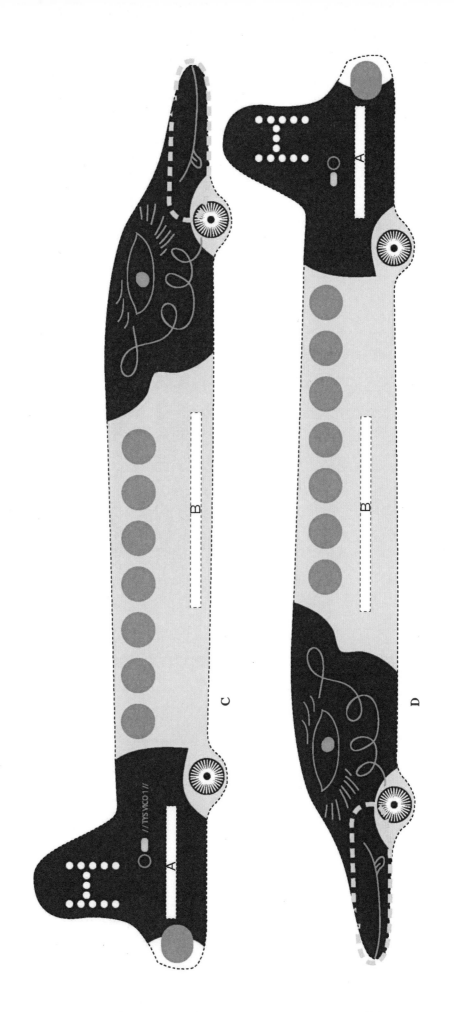

PERMANENTFOOD

DIY

PERMANENTFOOD

℗

Copy these logos on a color copy machine,
or download them from phaidon.com/diy,
and print in color. Scale to the size of the
magazine you made. Cut out and glue to
the cover.

Patterns or templates for the following projects
can be downloaded at 1:1 scale from phaidon.com/diy:

- Yves Béhar, Amplify, p.94
- Patricia Urquiola, Snap, p.106
- Pauline Deltour, Shoe Man, p.110
- Bernotat&Co, Apollo 11, p.146
- Jaime Hayon, Tys Vico 1, p. 150
- Steffen Kehrle, Station Wagon, p.190
- Maurizio Cattelan & Paola Manfrin, Permanent Food, p.198
- Piet Hein Eek, Edam Chair, p.202

Acknowledgments

We would like to thank all the designers who created projects for this book and made them available to us and to the public. We would also like to thank all the staff of *Süddeutsche Zeitung Magazin* who contributed to making the book.

Note on Safety

Please use tools with caution, according to the instructions, and always supervise children.

Photography

Myrzik und Jarisch, front and back cover, pp.87, 187, 191 / Sorin Morar pp.11, 23, 31, 35, 103, 115, 127, 151, 159, 167, 199 / Markus Jans p.14 / Fabian Zapatka pp.18, 19, 163 / Michael Barnett p.22 / Rory van Milligen p.26 / Faye Toogood p.27/ I & I Fotografie p.42 / Jäger & Jäger p.47 / Dirk Bruniecki p.46 / Raimund Koch pp.51, 55 / Chris Callis p.50 / Rainer Hosch p.54 / Attila Hartwig pp.58, 59, 83, 107, 131, 155, 171 / Ralf Zimmermann p.67 / Hedi Slimane p.70 / Molly Berman pp.71, 72 / Corentin Harbelot p.74 / Tobias Nickerl p.75 / Charlie Schuck p.78 / Gerhard Kellermann p.82 / Gisela Schenker p.90 / Mark Serr p.95 / Gao Yuan p.98 / Max Zambelli p.106 / Pauline Deltour p.111 / Franck Juery p.110 / Scottie Cameron p.119 / Lufe Gomez p.130 / Delfino Sisto Legnani p.134 / Horst Friedrichs p.139 / Jonathan Olivares Design Research p.142, 143 / Rogier Chang p.146 / Marleen Sleeuwits p.147 / Fabian Frinzel p.154 / Rob Overmeer p.174 / Stefan Botev p.175, 207 / Devendra Banhart p.178 / Francessca Lotti p.182 / Sabine Schweigert p.183 / Katrin Lautenbach p.186 / Julian Baumann p.190 / Iacopo Benassi pp.198, 199 (magazine cover)

All illustrations were designed and executed for this book by Claudia Klein, based on the instructions provided by each designer.

Phaidon Press Limited
Regent's Wharf
All Saints Street
London N1 9PA

Phaidon Press Inc.
65 Bleecker Street
New York, NY 10012

www.phaidon.com

First published 2015
© 2015 Phaidon Press Limited

ISBN 978 0 7148 7019 9

A CIP catalogue record for this book is available from the British Library.

Commissioning Editor: Emilia Terragni
Project Editor : Luisa de Miranda
Production Controller: Steve Bryant

Design: Thomas Kartsolis, Manuel Birnbacher, Sophie Chatellier, Ralf Zimmermann (picture editor)

Illustrations
Claudia Klein

Printed in Europe